GREGG SHORTHAND

A MANUEL FOR SHORTHAND

By
JOHN ROBERT GREGG

New and Revised Edition

The Gregg Publishing Company

NEW YORK   CHICAGO   BOSTON   SAN FRANCISCO   LONDON

I53-F-100

PRINTED IN THE UNITED STATES OF AMERICA

CONTENTS

CONTENTS

CONTENTS   V

vi   CONTENTS

PREFACE

In the Preface to the first edition of this system,
I said:

> The endeavor of the author has been to compile a
> system so simple as to be readily acquired by the humblest
> capacity and those possessed of little leisure, and yet rapid
> enough to reproduce verbatim the fastest oratory. In
> presenting his work to the public he asks for nothing
> beyond an impartial investigation, and with perfect con-
> fidence awaits the result.

The subsequent history of the system has justified
the confidence expressed at that time. Gregg Shorthand has demonstrated its superiority to the older systems in simplicity, legibility and speed—and there are
to-day nearly a million writers of the system. In beginning the preparation of this edition it was my inten-
tion to make some radical changes in the manner of
presenting the principles; but in proceeding with the
revision I was forced to the conclusion that it would
be a mistake to depart materially from the general plan
and form of the previous edition. No better evidence
of the popularity and success of the previous edition
could be given than the fact that, although nearly a
million copies of it have been sold, there has been very
little demand for revision except requests for the in-
clusion of those changes and improvements that have
been made in the course of the past few years.

This edition, then, retains the general plan and form
of the previous edition, but much of the material con-
tained in it is arranged in more logical sequence, and the
illustrations are chosen with greater care, with a view to
developing quickness in the application of its rules and
principles.   An attempt has been made to state some of
the rules more clearly than was done in the old book,
and to put them into language better adapted to the
comprehension of young students.

In the system itself few changes have been found
necessary or desirable.   Some new word-signs and exten-
sions of advanced principles have been introduced, but
all of these are in harmony with the fundamental principles of the system.   All of them have been subjected
to very careful trial in practical work before they have
been adopted.

In sending forth this book I desire to express my
heartfelt appreciation of the suggestions that have come
to me from writers, from reporters and from teachers
who are using the system in all parts of the world.
These suggestions have been of great service to me in
the preparation of this presentation of the system.

                    JOHN ROBERT GREGG.

New York, June 17, 1916.

About Gregg Shorthand

HISTORY.—Gregg Shorthand was first published in 1888, in two little paper-covered pamphlets, under the title, "Light-Line Phonography." Five years later, a revised and greatly improved edition was published under the title, "Gregg Shorthand." It was not until 1897, however, that the author was able to publish the system in *book* form.

To the student or writer of shorthand, there are few more interesting or inspiring stories of success than the story of the career of Gregg Shorthand in the twenty-seven years that have elapsed since its publication in book form; but a textbook is not a place for such a story. Today Gregg Shorthand is the standard system of America. It has been adopted exclusively in the public schools of 4633 cities and towns—more than ninety-two per cent of the public schools that teach shorthand. It has superseded the older systems, in the large majority of these cases, by formal action of the Boards of Education after careful investigation of the merit of the system. Its leadership in all other kinds of educational institutions is equally pronounced. This constitutes the highest educational endorsement a shorthand system has ever received.

WINS WORLD CHAMPIONSHIP THREE TIMES.—The history of Gregg Shorthand is a record of public triumphs. In the 1921 World's Championship Contest of the National Shorthand Reporters' Association, Mr. Albert Schneider * won first place, defeated three former champions, and established two world's records. He transcribed the 215-words-a-minute literary dictation with a net speed of 211.2 words a minute; accuracy, 98.32%. On the 200-words-a-minute dictation his accuracy percentage was 98.80; on the 240-words-a-minute dictation, 98.17; on the 280-words-a-minute dictation, 96.84.

In transcribing five five-minute highest speed dictations—175, 200, 215, 240, and 280 words a minute—*in the time allotted for the three championship dictations,* Mr. Schneider gave the most remarkable demonstration of his transcribing ability in the history of the shorthand contests, and proved again the wonderful legibility of Gregg Shorthand.

---

*Mr. Schneider is now a member of the official shorthand reporting staff of the Congress of the United States, winning the position in an examination in which thirty-five well-known reporters competed.

Writers of Gregg Shorthand won first, second, and third places in the World's Championship Contest of the National Shorthand Reporters' Association in 1923. Mr. Charles L. Swem,* winner, established a world's record on the 200-words-a-minute dictation, making but two errors; accuracy, 99.79%. On the 240-words-a-minute dictation, his accuracy was 98.49%; on the 280 dictation, 99.36%. Second place was won by Mr. Albert Schneider, a Gregg writer, the 1921 champion. His average accuracy was 98.80%. Third place was won by a seventeen-year-old Gregg writer, Mr. Martin Dupraw, with an accuracy of 98.76%. *First place in accuracy in every dictation was won by a writer of Gregg Shorthand.*

In the 1924 World's Championship, Mr. Swem was again the victor, defeating, among others, Mr. Nathan Behrin, Supreme Court stenographer of New York City, winner of many championships. Third place was won by Mr. Dupraw. Mr. Swem's accuracy on the three dictations was 99.23%.

Gregg Shorthand is the only system that has produced two different writers to win the world championship in the contests of the National Shorthand Reporters' Association.

WINS NEW YORK STATE SHORTHAND CHAMPIONSHIP.—In the contest of the New York State Shorthand Reporters' Association, December, 1924, Mr. Martin J. Dupraw won first place and the Bottome Cup; Mr. Nathan Behrin, Supreme Court reporter, New York City, second; and Mr. Harvey Forbes, Supreme Court reporter, Buffalo, New York, third. Mr. Dupraw made twelve errors in transcribing the five-minute dictations at 200 and 280 words a minute; average accuracy, 99.5%. Mr. Behrin made twenty-eight errors; average accuracy, 98.8%.

AWARDED MEDAL OF HONOR AT PANAMA-PACIFIC EXPOSITION.— At the Panama-Pacific International Exposition, in 1915, Gregg Shorthand was awarded the Medal of Honor, the highest award

---

*Governor Woodrow Wilson selected Mr. Swem as his official reporter in his campaign for the Presidency. Mr. Swem was Personal Secretary and Official Reporter to President Wilson for eight years. Mr. Swem began the study of Gregg Shorthand in a night school in September, 1908, when working as an office boy. He was twenty years of age when he received the appointment at the White House. In the 1924 examination for the position of Supreme Court stenographer in the State of New York, Mr. Swem won first place in a field of 150 candidates.

ever granted a system of shorthand by any Exposition and the only award ever granted which was based on the results accomplished by students in a model school conducted under the observation of the International Jury of Awards.

PRINCIPLES OF THE SYSTEM.—Needless to say, Gregg Shorthand is a radical departure from the old lines of shorthand construction, for it is only by a radical departure that such marked superiority in results can be accomplished.

The following synopsis will enable the reader to understand the leading features of the system:

(1) NO COMPULSORY THICKENING.—May be written either light or heavy.

(2) WRITTEN ON THE SLOPE OF LONGHAND, thus securing a uniform manual movement.

(3) POSITION WRITING ABOLISHED.—May be written on unruled paper, and in one straight line.

(4) VOWELS AND CONSONANTS ARE JOINED, and follow each other in their natural order.

(5) ANGLES ARE RARE.—Curves predominate.

As in ordinary writing

This brief synopsis will suffice to show that the aim of the author has been to adhere to those natural principles which govern ordinary writing. By a practical combination of these elements as a foundation, the system secures to the writer, *with very little practice*, that perfect command of the characters which is productive of the best results, and is only obtained by years of persistent, painstaking practice if the old geometric systems are employed.

TO SUM UP:

EASY TO LEARN.—Gregg Shorthand may be learned in from one-third to one-half the time required by the old systems. The records made by its writers prove this beyond all question.

EASY TO READ.—Gregg Shorthand is the most legible shorthand in existence. In the public shorthand speed contests, writers of the system have established the *highest official world's records for accuracy* of transcripts on solid, difficult matter. These records were made in competition with experienced reporters who used the older systems, and in contests conducted by reporters and teachers who wrote such systems. (Full particulars of these contests will be sent by the publishers on application.) Manifestly, the insertion of the vowels, the absence of shading, the elimination of position-writing and the elimination of the minute distinctions of form necessary in the old systems, all contribute to legibility.

EASY TO WRITE.—The easy, natural appearance of the writing in Gregg Shorthand appeals to every impartial investigator. The absence of distinctions between light and heavy characters, the continuous run of the writing along one line, as in longhand, instead of constant changes of position—now *on* the line, then *above* the line, and then, perhaps, *through* or *below* the line—will be noticed at a first glance. Next, the investigator will probably attribute much of the natural, pleasing appearance of the writing to that uniform slant of the writing, with which both hand and eye are familiar. Only those who have had previous experience with shorthand, however, will be able to appreciate fully how much elimination of numerous dots and dashes—minute marks that have to be placed with great precision alongside the strokes—contributes to easy, continuous, effortless writing.

SUPERIOR IN SPEED POSSIBILITIES.—Writers of Gregg Shorthand have demonstrated in public speed contests, under the most trying conditions, that the system has greater speed possibilities than any other system. A boy of nineteen (who began the study of Gregg Shorthand in a night school less than four years previously) established a record of 268 words a minute net for five minutes, defeating three former champions and eighteen other experienced and capable reporters. The contest committee consisted of seven shorthand reporters, all of whom were writers of other systems. When a mere boy can do this, after such a brief experience, there can be no question that this system of shorthand possesses greater speed possibilities than any of the older systems.

A TALK WITH THE BEGINNER

Success in any study depends largely upon the *interest* taken in that particular subject by the student. This being the case, we earnestly hope that you will realize at the very outset that shorthand can be made an intensely fascinating study. Cultivate a love for it. Think of it as the highest form of writing, which is itself the greatest invention of man. Be proud that you can record the language in graceful lines and curves. Aim constantly to acquire artistic skill in executing those lines and curves. You *can*, if you *will*, make the study of shorthand a perfect joy instead of a task. Its possession has been coveted by the wisest of men and women, for it is not only a practical instrument in commercial work, but a much prized and valuable accomplishment and a means of mental culture.

BE THOROUGH.—Skill in anything is attained by repetition; therefore do not shirk the careful, painstaking practice on the elementary forms given in the Manual. Write each outline many times, and aim always at the attainment of ease and exactness in execution.

Your future success depends to a very large extent on the way you do your work now. In order that your progress may be sure and rapid, master each lesson before you proceed with the next.

At first, write slowly and carefully; aim at accuracy rather than speed, but do not *draw* the characters. You must understand at the outset that shorthand must be *written;* but you must also impress upon your mind that whatever you write you must read, hence the necessity for good penmanship. As skill in executing the movements is obtained, the speed may be increased until the forms are written rapidly. Some attention should be given to acquiring a capacity for writing *individual* outlines rapidly without hesitation, and with a free movement of the hand.

Aim to acquire a smooth style of writing; execute each character with an easy, *continuous* motion of the pen, and pass directly to the next without unnecessary movements. A halting, jerky movement is fatal to speed, and may be almost always traced to

xiii

indecision, caused by unfamiliarity with the forms. At first carefully analyze the words. To do this it is, of course, necessary for you to think of them in detail; but after you have determined the correct outline, practice it and think of it as a *whole*.

Facility in the use of shorthand depends largely upon the stock of outlines you have at your ready command. Note the use of that word *ready*. This means that you should master all the forms given in the Manual by writing them many times. This will not only impress the forms on your mind so that you will not have any hesitation in recalling them, but will give you facility in writing them. In shorthand it is not sufficient to *know* how to write a word—you must not only know the form but be able to write it quickly. Hence the necessity for much *repetition practice* in writing the forms.

If, in addition to the words given in the Manual, you can add to your stock of outlines other words written under the same principles you will have gained a great deal—will have laid a broader foundation for advanced work which will lessen the time required to attain efficiency.

DEVOTE MUCH TIME TO READING WELL-WRITTEN SHORTHAND. —By doing this you will become not only a fluent reader, but you will enlarge your writing vocabulary. Unconsciously you will imitate in your own work the easy execution of the forms shown in the printed plates. All expert writers have devoted much time to reading shorthand.

In addition to the work outlined in this Manual, we strongly recommend the use of the exercises given each month in the Learners' Department of the *Gregg Writer*. These exercises can be used with great advantage from the very first lesson. Each number contains many helpful suggestions, and a number of shorthand pages that afford valuable exercises in reading and writing for students at all stages of advancement.

DON'T GET DISCOURAGED.—The complete mastery of shorthand and typewriting is worthy of your best efforts, and if you devote yourself earnestly to that work there can be no such thing as failure

THE UNITED STATES OF AMERICA
PANAMA-PACIFIC INTERNATIONAL EXPOSITION
SAN FRANCISCO, MCMXV.

ARTS & SCIENCE · MANUFACTURES · TRANSPORTATION

EDUCATION · AGRICULTURE · MINING

CELEBRATING THE OPENING OF THE PANAMA CANAL
THE INTERNATIONAL JURY OF AWARDS HAS CONFERRED A

MEDAL OF HONOR

upon

THE GREGG PUBLISHING COMPANY

PANAMA

xv

The Alphabet of Gregg Shorthand

CONSONANTS

Written forward:

K	G	R	L	N	M	T	D	TH

Written downward:

P	B	F	V	CH	J	S	SH

H	NG	NK

(A dot)

VOWELS

A-group

Short	ă as in	cat	◯
Medium	ä " "	calm	◯
Long	ā " "	came	◯

O-group

Short	ŏ as in	hot	◡
Medium	aw " "	audit	◡
Long	ō " "	ode	◡

E-group

Short	ĭ as in	din	o
Medium	ĕ " "	den	o
Long	ē " "	dean	o

OO-group

Short	ŭ as in	tuck	⌒
Medium	ŏŏ " "	took	⌒
Long	ōō " "	doom	⌒

DIPHTHONGS

	Composed of		
ū	ē-ōō	as in unit	
ow	ä-ōō	" " owl	

	Composed of		
oi	aw-ē	as in oil	
ī	ä-ē	" " isle	

xvi

FIRST LESSON

1. Shorthand is written by *sound;* thus *aim* is written
ăm (iong sound of *a*), *cat* is written *kăt, knee* is written *nē.*

Consonants

2. The alphabet should be mastered in sections, as
given in these lessons. It will be noticed that the consonants are arranged in pairs, according to their affinity
of sound, and are distinguished by a difference in length.
There is no absolute standard as to length, as the characters, being founded on ordinary writing, vary in size,
slant, etc., according to the personal habits of the writer.
The size of the characters given in this manual will be a
safe standard to adopt.   The characters for the consonants in this lesson are derived from an elliptical figure,
thus:

K	G	R	L	N	M	T	D	H

NOTE: All these characters are written *forward* from left to right, and T, D
struck *upwards* from the line of writing. The G given in this lesson is called *gay,*
being the hard sound as in *game, get,* and not the soft sound heard in *gem,*
magic. The aspirate H is indicated by a dot placed over the vowel. The student
should practice all these characters until he can write them without the slightest
hesitation.

1

VOWELS

3. In writing by sound there are twelve distinct vowels, which are arranged in four groups, and three closely related sounds are placed in each group. In this lesson we have the first two groups, which for convenience are named the "A" group and the "E" group.

4. The *short* sound of *a*, as heard in *cat, ran*, is expressed by the large circle; the *medium* sound, as heard in *calm, ark*, is expressed by the large circle with a dot beneath the circle; the *long* sound, as heard in *ate, may*, is expressed by the large circle with a dash beneath the circle.

ă	○	*as in*	mat	m ă t	
ä	○	*as in*	calm	k ä m	
ā	○	*as in*	gate	g ā t	

5. The *short* sound of *i*, as heard in *din, rid* (not the long sound of *i*, heard in *dine, ride*), is expressed by the small circle; the sound of *e*, as heard in *get, net*, is expressed by the small circle with a dot beneath the circle; the *long* sound of *e*, as heard in *me, eat*, is expressed by the small circle with a dash beneath the circle.

ĭ	o	*as in*	knit	n ĭ t	
ĕ	o	*as in*	net	n ĕ t	
ė	o	*as in*	neat	n ē t	

Note: The dot and dash are useful to indicate the exact vowel sounds in unfamiliar or in isolated words, but otherwise they are seldom used.

RULES FOR JOINING CIRCLES

6. The circle is written on the *inside of curves*, and on the *outside of angles*.

Inside Curves

eke	ē k		era	ē r a	
key	k ē		rat	r ă t	
ale	ā l		take	t ā k	

Outside Angles

team	t ē m		rail	r ā l	
meet	m ē t		gain	g ā n	

7. Before or after straight lines, or between two straight lines running in the same direction, the circle is written forward—as the hands of a clock move.

Before   *After*

aim	ā m		me	m ē	
hat	h ă t		day	d ā	

Between

mean	m ē n		deed	d ē d	

8. Between two reverse curves the circle is turned on the back of the first curve.

kill	k ĭ l		gear	g ē r	
wreck	r ĕ k		lake	l ā k	

9. The following list of words should now be copied. In doing this, particular attention must be paid to the *sounds* of each word. If the student will repeat the sounds as he writes the word, it will help to impress the forms upon his memory and at the same time familiarize him with the process of note-taking.

GENERAL EXERCISE

knee	n ē		tact	t ă k t	
keen	k ē n		tray	t r ā	
kick	k ĭ k		train	t r ā n	
ache	ā k		treat	t r ē t	
acre	ā k r		nail	n ā l	
acme	a k m ē		tale	t ā l	
neck	n ĕ k		lay	l ā	
cake	k ā k		deem	d ē m	
ark	ä r k		rim	r ĭ m	
eat	ē t		reed	' r ē d	
kit	k ĭ t		arid	a r ĭ d	
hit	h ĭ t		rainy	r ā n ĭ	
had	h ă d		hack	h ă k	

eddy	ĕ d ĭ		ill	ĭ l
writ	r ĭ t		hill	h ĭ l
came	k ā m		mill	m ĭ l
creed	k r ē d		attic	ă t ĭ k
cream	k r ĕ m		tickle	t ĭ k l
merry	m ĕ r ĭ		ticket	t ĭ k ĕ t
lane	l ā n		trick	t r ĭ k
lamb	l ă m		deck	d ĕ k
lady	l ā d ĭ		deacon	d ē k n
rack	r ă k		decay	d ē k ā
ready	r ĕ d ĭ		reel	r ē l
maim	m ā m		gray	g r ā
grim	g r ĭ m		eagle	ē g l
rally	r ă l ĭ		arena	a r ē n a
get	g ĕ t		narrate	n ă r ā t
rig	r ĭ g		marine	m a r ē n
linen	l ĭ n ĕ n		hatred	h ā t r ĕ d
drama	d r ä m a		camera	k ă m ĕ r a
rag	r ă g		tyranny	t ĭ r a n ĭ
lick	l ĭ k		etiquette	ĕ t ĭ k ĕ t

SIMPLE WORD-SIGNS

10. A large proportion of all written and spoken language is made up of a few simple words. For such words brief forms called word-signs are provided. Those given here should be memorized immediately:

can	⌒	in, not	—	he	ₒ
go, good	⌒⌒	am more	——	I	◯
are, our	⌣—	ət, it	╱	a, an (dot)	·
well, will	⌣—⌣	would	╱	the (th)	⌒

up

PHRASE-WRITING

11. The joining of simple words is a great help to speed in writing shorthand, but it is a difficult art to acquire if its acquirement be deferred until the habit has been formed of writing common words separately. The student should, therefore, practice it diligently from the very beginning of his study. For such practice the simple phrases here given will serve as models:

in the	⌒	I would	⌒	it will not	⌒
I can	⌒	I am	⌒—	I can not	⌒
I will	⌐⌣	at the	╱	in our	⌣—
would not	╱	it will	⌣—	can the	⌣—

PUNCTUATION, ETC.

12. The *period* is expressed by ⌣, the end of a *paragraph* by >, the *dash* by ═, the *hyphen* by ⌀ (two short dashes struck upward), and the *interrogation* by ×. Capitals and proper names may be indicated by two short dashes under the outline. The parentheses may be expressed by the ordinary marks with short dashes through them ⟨ ⟩. Other punctuation marks are written in the usual way.

READING EXERCISE

WRITING EXERCISE

1. Ellen Terry read the drama well.
2. Helen Keller can read in-the-dark.
3. The rain will make the day dreary.
4. The enemy may make an attack in-the rear.
5. The League team will meet at-the Arena.

SECOND LESSON

THE DOWNWARD CHARACTERS

13. The characters for the consonants in this lesson are derived from another elliptical figure; thus

P	B	F	V	CH	J	SH

NOTES: All these characters are written downwards. CH is pronounced *chay*, not *see-aitch*; and SH is called *ish*, not *es-aitch*. SH is a mere tick.
The following memory aids will be helpful:

14. In the writing of F, V, a rather vertical inclination is desirable in order that the curve may join easily with other characters. In forming the combinations *fr, fl*, it is not necessary to make an angle. The motion is just the same as in writing a part of Y in longhand; thus

fig	f ĭ g		free	f r ē	
vain	v ā n		frame	f r ā m	
fail	f ā l		flash	f l ă sh	

8

15. The circle may assume the form of a loop where more convenient.

dash	d ă sh		cheat	ch ē t	
fame	f ā m		lap	l ă p	

16. Between an oblique curve—such as P, B, F, V— and a straight line, the circle is placed on the outside.

palm	p ä m		Dave	d ā v	
beat	b ē t		knave	n ā v	

17. The base of the first consonant of a word rests on the line of writing.

map	m ă p		fetch	f ĕ ch	
cave	k ā v		chief	ch ē f	

18. The following words illustrate the application of the rules for joining circles to the consonants given in this lesson:

Inside Curves (Par. 6).

Outside Angles (Par. 6).

Joined to Straight Lines (Par. 7).

. *Between Reverse Curves* (Par. 8).

Between Oblique Curves and Straight Lines (Par. 16).

GENERAL EXERCISE

edge	ĕ j		jig	j ĭ g	
able	ā b l		apple	ă p l	
fear	f ē r		peal	p ē l	
beer	b ē r		appeal	ă p ē l	
fish	f ĭ sh		cheap	ch ē p	
feed	f ē d		chap	ch ă p	
play	p l ā		beak	b ē k	
cheek	ch ē k		back	b ă k	
reap	r ē p		beam	b ē m	
peep	p ē p		balm	b ä m	
Jap	j ă p		chain	ch ā n	
nap	n ă p		catch	k ă ch	
cab	k ă b		shake	sh ā k	
peach	p ē ch		shame	sh ā m	
preach	p r ē ch		bread	b r ĕ d	
tab	t ă b		bridge	b r ĭ j	
gem	j ĕ m		shave	sh ā v	
pale	p ā l		fray	f r ā	
sherry	sh ĕ r ĭ		feel	f ē l	

ledge	l ĕ j		Arab	ă r a b	
allege	ă l ĕ j		chill	ch ĭ l	
pledge	p l ĕ j		Jack	j ă k	
nib	n ĭ b		rage	r ā j	
brief	b r ē f		page	p ā j	
chin	ch ĭ n		vague	v ā g	
calf	k ä f		dip	d ĭ p	
rave	r ā v		rich	r ĭ ch	
grave	g r ā v		navy	n ā v ĭ	
shade	sh ā d		cliff	k l ĭ f	
half	h ä f		shaggy	sh ă g ĭ	
badge	b ă j		vim	v ĭ m	
brain	b r ā n		abate	a b ā t	
valid	v ă l ĭ d		heavy	h ĕ v ĭ	
trap	t r ă p		Java	j ä v a	
crash	k r ă sh		parish	p ă r ĭ sh	
trash	t r ă sh		palate	p ă l a t	
beef	b ē f		flinch	f l ĭ n ch	
brave	b r ā v		beetle	b ē t l	
hitch	h ĭ ch		avail	ă v ā l	

WORD-SIGNS AND PHRASES

put		let, letter	
be, but, by		little	
been, bound		market, Mr.	
before, behalf		reply	
belief, believe		represent	
for		teach	
form, from		check	
have		for the	
change, which		I have	
shall, ship		I have not	
about		in which	
after		I shall	
ever-y		I shall not	
any		I shall have	
name		from the	
give-n		would be	
gave		in reply	
please		please ship	

NOTE: The rule given in Par. 17 applies to phrases.

READING EXERCISE

WRITING EXERCISE

1. The maid will-be at-the market every day.
2. Phoebe Cary will teach her French.
3. The team will-be ready for-the match game.
4. Henry came back from-the navy after he had achieved fame.
5. The range in-the kitchen will bake good bread.
6. Jennie will-have the meal ready in about an hour.
7. Please pay for-the ticket in cash for I-can-not take a check.

THIRD LESSON

THE O-HOOK

19. The lower part of the elliptical figure *𝒪ₒ* (called the *o-hook*) represents the short sound of *o*, as heard in *hot, top;* the hook with a dot beneath it expresses the sound of *aw*, as in *awe, law;* the hook with a short dash beneath it expresses the long sound of *o*, as in *owe, no.*

ŏ	ʋ	*as in*	rot	r ŏ t	
aw	ɤ	*as in*	raw	r aw	
ō	ɤ	*as in*	wrote	r ō t	

GENERAL EXERCISE

hot	h ŏ t		Shaw	sh aw	
ought	aw t		shawl	sh aw l	
taught	t aw t		show	sh ō	
odd	ŏ d		shoal	sh ō l	
nod	n ŏ d		toad	t ō d	
Maud	m aw d		foe	f ō	
mode	m ō d		foam	f ō m	

14

loaf	l ō f		paw	p aw	
cope	k ō p		pawn	p aw n	
coach	k ō ch		jaw	j aw	
rod	r ŏ d		dodge	d ŏ j	
blow	b l ō		lodge	l ŏ j	
botch	b ŏ ch		talk	t aw k	
hobby	h ŏ b ĭ		broad	b r aw d	
fraud	f r aw d		dough	d ō	
wrought	r aw t		Jove	j ō v	
dot	d ŏ t		obey	ō b ā	
ball	b aw l		hope	h ō p	
hog	h ŏ g		fop	f ŏ p	
blot	b l ŏ t		chop	ch ŏ p	
rogue	r ō g		Paul	p aw l	
pillow	p ĭ l ō		pole	p ō l	
shallow	sh ă l ō		beau	b ō	
elbow	ĕ l b ō		arrow	ă r ō	
rope	r ō p		John	j ŏ n	
polo	p ō l ō		bone	b ō n	
bore	b ō r		motto	m ŏ t ō	

20. The O-hook is placed on its side *before* N, M, R, L, except when preceded by a downward character, as in *bore, bone, pole, foam, John.*

on	ŏ n		hall	h aw l	
or	aw r		dome	d ō m	
moan	m ō n		Nome	n ō m	

GENERAL EXERCISE

nor	n aw r		home	h ō m	
orb	aw r b		flown	f l ō n	
own	ō n		knoll	n ō l	
whole	h ō l		drawn	d r aw n	
hollow	h ŏ l ō		blown	b l ō n	
aroma	a r ō m a		tone	t ō n	
core	k ō r		atone	a t ō n	
known	n ō n		door	d ō r	
roam	r ō m		adore	a d ō r	
roll	r ō l		loan	l ō n	
comb	k ō m		alone	a l ō n	
coal	k ō l		mole	m ō l	
omit	ō m ĭ t		dawn	d aw n	

goal	g ō l		holy	h ō l ĭ	
tall	t aw l		Nora	n ō r a	
brawny	b r aw n ĭ		Cora	k ō r a	

WORD-SIGNS AND PHRASES

all		told	
beyond		very	
body		of the	
call		of all	
care		of which	
company, keep		of our	
fall, fellow		in favor	
far, favor		in our favor	
friend-ly		on the	
glad		on our	
judge		on which	
most		on which the	
of		in regard	
public, publish		I told	
real, regard		on behalf	

Reading Exercise

Writing Exercise

1. The team will haul the heavy load of coal.
2. Judge Lodge would-not keep the letter from-the public.
3. He will-pay for-the lot if Mr. Cone will take a check drawn in-our-favor.
4. I-can-not very well follow the form given in-the letter.
5. After the ball game Laura came home in-the launch.
6. The good ship Jane dashed on a rock, but all the people reached the shore.

FOURTH LESSON

THE OO-HOOK

21. The upper part of the small elliptical figure ⌒ (called the *oo-hook*) represents the short sound of *u*, heard in *hum, dumb* (not the long *u* heard in *use*, which will be given later); the hook with a dot beneath it expresses the sound of *oo*, as in *took, foot*; the hook with a short dash beneath it expresses the long *oo*, as in *doom, boom*.

ŭ	⌒	*as in*	tuck	t ŭ k	
ŏŏ	⌒	*as in*	took	t ŏŏ k	
ōō	⌒	*as in*	tomb	t ōō m	

GENERAL EXERCISE

hut	h ŭ t		doom	d ōō m	
tug	t ŭ g		shove	sh ŭ v	
shut	sh ŭ t		hug	h ŭ g	
shoot	sh ōō t		rut	r ŭ t	
to	t ŏŏ		shoe	sh ōō	
do	d ōō		shook	sh ŏŏ k	

19

foot	f o͞o t		up	ŭ p	
cuff	k ŭ f		dug	d ŭ g	
hush	h ŭ sh		jug	j ŭ g	
gush	g ŭ sh		fudge	f ŭ j	
honey	h ŭ n ĭ		huff	h ŭ f	
duck	d ŭ k		pool	p o͞o l	
hood	h o͝o d		fool	f o͞o l	
hook	h o͝o k		toot	t o͞o t	
dove	d ŭ v		oven	ŭ v n	
puff	p ŭ f		tough	t ŭ f	
who	h o͞o		ruddy	r ŭ d ĭ	
whom	h o͞o m		chuckle	ch ŭ k l	
huddle	h ŭ d l		boom	b o͞o m	
tattoo	t ă t o͞o		lucky	l ŭ k ĭ	

22. The OO-hook is always placed on its side *after* N or M; it is also placed on its side *after* K or G *when followed by* R or L.

nun	n ŭ n		mug	m ŭ g	
mud	m ŭ d		mood	m o͞o d	
muff	m ŭ f		cool	k o͞o l	
moon	m o͞o n		gull	g ŭ l	

REVIEW EXERCISE ON BOTH HOOKS

hot	h ŏ t		loam	l ō m	
hut	h ŭ t		loom	l ōō m	
home	h ō m		rot	r ŏ t	
hum	h ŭ m		rut	r ŭ t	
moan	m ō n		bone	b ō n	
moon	m ōō n		boon	b ōō n	
mode	m ō d		coach	k ō ch	
mood	m ōō d		gush	g ŭ sh	
dome	d ō m		coal	k ō l	
doom	d ōō m		cull	k ŭ l	

W AND Y

23. When followed by a vowel, W has the sound of ōō, as ōō-ā-t—*wait*. W is therefore expressed by the oo-hook.

we	w ē		wall	w aw l	
weave	w ē v		woe	w ō	
wait	w ā t		wool	w ŏŏ l	

24. In the body of a word it is generally more convenient to express *w* by a horizontal dash under the vowel, but this dash may often be omitted.

twig	t w ĭ g		equity	ĕ k w ĭ t ĭ	
twin	t w ĭ n		dwell	d w ĕ l	
quick	k w ĭ k		headway	h ĕ d w ā	

25. In words beginning with *a-h* or *a-w*, followed by a vowel, *a* is expressed by a dot placed on the line close to the next character.

ahead	a h ĕ d		awake	a w ā k	
away	a w ā		ahem	a h ĕ m	

26. Wh is pronounced *hw*, as h-w-ē-l — *wheel*, hence the dot for *h* should be written first.

whit	hw ĭ t		whack	hw ă k	
whig	hw ĭ g		whim	hw ĭ m	

27. Y is equivalent to ē, as ē-ō-r — *yore*, and is therefore represented by the small circle.

yacht	y ŏ t		yore	y ō r	
yawn	y aw n		yawl	y aw l	

NOTE: When the combination *yo* or *yaw* precedes R or L, the hook is not placed on its side.

28. At the beginning of a word *yĭ* or *ye* is expressed by a small loop, and *ya* by a large loop.   When neces-

sary to denote the exact shade of vowel sound, the dot
or dash is placed beneath the loop.

ye	yē		yet	yĕ t	
yea	yā		yellow	yĕ l ō	
year	yē r		Yale	yā l	

GENERAL EXERCISE

way	w ā		acquit	ă k w ĭ t	
wave	w ā v		quail	k w ā l	
wade	w ā d		Broadway	b r aw d w ā	
wake	w ā k		roadway	r ō d w ā	
wage	w ā j		await	a w ā t	
weed	w ē d		awoke	a w ō k	
widow	w ĭ d ō		wheel	hw ē l	
weep	w ē p		wheat	hw ē t	
walk	w aw k		whip	hw ĭ p	
wash	w ŏ sh		whiff	hw ĭ f	
watch	w ŏ ch		yam	yă m	
wove	w ō v		Yarrow	yă r ō	
quack	k w ă k		yoke	y ō k	

WORD-SIGNS AND PHRASES

above		of your	
become, book		to you	
could		do you	
full-y		you have	
great		you have not	
look		we have	
move		we have not	
much		you can not	
should		we can not	
sure-ly		we will	
upon		from you	
work		your letter	
world		if you have	
yes		if you will	
you, your		if you can	

W is omitted in the following words:

week		when	
were		what	
where		won-one	

READING EXERCISE

WRITING EXERCISE

1. The wheel of-the wagon caught in a rut of-the rough road.
2. The pony ran away but the groom caught him.
3. Edwin should-have told you about-the affair before the letter reached you.
4. You-may do the work in your own way if-you-are sure you-can do it well.
5. The mud in-the road will-reach up to-the hub of-the wagon wheel.

FIFTH LESSON

S AND TH

29. From the small elliptical figure given in the last lesson *∅* two small curves are obtained which are written downwards to express the very common letter S, and upwards to express Th.

S	TH
(or *)*	*⌒* or *⁄*
down	*up*

NOTE: It is very important to keep steadily in mind that the curves for S are written *downwards*, while those for TH are written *upwards* and at a greater inclination. The following is a useful memory aid:

RULES FOR JOINING S AND TH

30. When S is joined to a curve, the S is written in the same direction as the curve to which it is joined, thus securing a *uniform movement*. A circle vowel occurring at the joining does not affect the application of this rule.

spray		safe		makes	
reaps		face		case	
pass		skate		slay	
sphere		sick		sales	

NOTE: When S precedes a down stroke, the base of the *down stroke* rests on the line.

26

31. When S is joined to T, D, N, M, the S is used which forms a sharp angle. A circle vowel occurring at the joining does not affect the application of this rule

stay		odds		smack	
set		days		same	
nets		snow		leans	
said		seen		knees	

32. When S is joined to Sh, Ch, J, the S is used which is written with the clockwise movement—called the "comma S."

sash		sage		chess	

33. In words consisting of S or Th, or both, and a *circle* vowel, S or Th should be written with the clockwise movement.

Circle and S		Circle and Th		Combinations	
as		heath		these	
see		hath		sees	
essay		thee		Seth	

34. The clockwise Th is given the preference, but when joined to O, R, L, the other form is used.

thick		though		moth	
theme		throw		earth	
doth		athlete		health	

35. In words beginning with *so*, the "comma S" is used.

so		soul		soap	
sorrow		sofa		sod	

36. The combination *us* is written without an angle at the beginning of words, or when it follows a down stroke or K, G.

us		fuss		gracious	
bus		gust		vicious	

37. Z is represented by the sign for S, but an oblique dash marks the distinction in isolated words. If necessary, the Th heard in *breathe* may be distinguished from the sound heard in *breath* in the same manner.

gas		face		breath	
gaze		phase		breathe	

NOTE: The sound of *zh*, heard in *azure, rouge, garage*, may be distinguished from *sh* by the oblique dash, but this is necessary only where it is desired to mark the precise sounds of foreign words.

38. The letter X may be expressed at the end, or in the body of words, (but not at the beginning), by a slight modification of the curve for S, as shown in the following examples:

mix		coax		tax	
box		fix		lax	

39. The sound of Ng, heard in *long*, is expressed by N written in a slightly downward direction; and Nk (which is sounded *ngk*, as *rang-k—rank*) by a longer sign.

rang		sing		king	
rank		sink		kink	

SIMPLE PREFIXES AND SUFFIXES

40. The prefixes *con*, *com*, *coun* are expressed by K, and the vowel is omitted in the prefixes *en*, *in*, *un*, *em*, *im* when the prefix is followed by a *consonant*. The prefix *ex* is expressed by *es*.

condole		infancy		impress	
convey		envy		extol	
compass		emboss		explode	

41. The suffix *ing* or *thing* is expressed by a dot placed beneath or close to the preceding letter; *ings* is expressed by S in the same place, the S being written contrary to the hands-of-a-clock movement.

being		singing		anything	
doing		making		sayings	
ringing		everything		readings	

42. The suffix *ly* is expressed by the small circle, and *ily, ally* by a loop.

only	⌐o	calmly	⌐o	prettily	⌐o
early	⌐	readily	⌐	totally	⌐

43. The suffix *tion, sion* (*shun*) is expressed by SH.

nation	⌐	session	⌐	action	⌐
oration	⌐	motion	⌐	fashion	⌐

GENERAL EXERCISE

say	⌐	guess	⌐	link	⌐
seem	⌐	chase	⌐	throat	⌐
save	⌐	sleepy	⌐	both	⌐
sap	⌐	serene	⌐	booth	⌐
solemn	⌐	steel	⌐	gang	⌐
scratch	⌐	stray	⌐	thief	⌐
scream	⌐	city	⌐	death	⌐
scrip	⌐	snake	⌐	swear	⌐
score	⌐	smash	⌐	switch	⌐
hymns	⌐	smith	⌐	sweet	⌐
miss	⌐	fasten	⌐	swim	⌐

NOTE: When *sw* is followed by T, D, N, or M, the *w* is expressed by the hook.

trace	salad	loath
terrace	threat	thud
shoes	throne	preface
shows	myth	spring
husky	wrong	*con*done
dusky	acid	*com*plex
hustle	bath	*con*cave
audacious	wing	*com*bat
zealous	zero	*coun*ty
efface	siege	*en*rich
ethics	thus	*in*famous
hasty	suffix	*un*fit
sabre	elixir	rela*tion*
saucy	applause	expres*sion*
essays	stab	*in*va*sion*
Jessie	sedate	shipp*ing*
sprain	theft	feel*ings*
elapse	sashes	thick*ly*
story	sober	brut*ally*
sparrow	plank	craft*ily*

Word-Signs and Phrases

ask		than, then	
business		that	
cause, because		their, there	
course		them	
desire		they	
else, list		thing, think	
inclose		this	
instan-$_{ce}^{t}$		those	
is, his		was	
long		is the	
must		is this	
next		is there	
other		there is	
receive		this is	
some		in these	
soon		for that	
speak, speech		he was	
state		there was	
such		in such	

READING EXERCISE

[shorthand notation]

WRITING EXERCISE

1. The book of essays by John Burroughs was-given a long notice in-the papers.

2. I-think that such a motion was made early in-the session.

3. I-shall-not wait for a letter from Mr. King as-the book is on-the press.

4. We-inclose a list of things which we-shall need very soon.

5. The speech by Nicholas Murray Butler was on-the ethics of teaching.

SIXTH LESSON

DIPHTHONGS

44. A pure diphthong is the union in one syllable of two simple vowels uttered in rapid succession. The diphthongs are therefore expressed by joining the circles and hooks representing the vowels of which they are composed.

ū		*as in*	fume	f ū m	
ow		*as in*	now	n ow	
oi		*as in*	oil	oi l	
ī		*as in*	die	d ī	

NOTE: The diphthong *ū* is a combination of *ē* and *ōō; ow,* of *ä* and *ōō; oi,* of *aw* and *ē.* The sign for the diphthong *ī* is a large circle with an indentation — resembling a combination of *ŭ* and *ē,* which, if uttered in rapid succession, yield a sound almost equivalent to *ī.* This sign for *ī* is generally called "the broken circle."

GENERAL EXERCISE

hue	h ū		fine	f ī n	
feud	f ū d		huge	h ū j	
cow	k ow		mute	m ū t	
toy	t oi		bough	b ow	
annoy	a n oi		Hoyle	h oi l	
sky	s k ī		try	t r ī	

34

word	sounds		word	sounds	
unique	ū n ē k		thy	th ī	
ounce	ow n s		humid	h ū m ĭ d	
toil	t oi l		sigh	s ī	
ripe	r ī p		scout	s k ow t	
youth	ū th		Nile	n ī l	
thou	th ow		vow	v ow	
mine	m ī n		price	p r ī s	
Roy	r oi		rhyme	r ī m	
cue	k ū		apply	ă p l ī	
guide	g ī d		tile	t ī l	
alloy	ă l oi		comply	*com* p l ī	
chime	ch ī m		invite	*in* v ī t	
adjoin	a j oi n		enjoy	*en* j oi	
fight	f ī t		impugn	*im* p ū n	
mouth	m ow th		exude	*ex* ū d	
noise	n oi s		mightily	m ī t *ily*	

NOTES: (a) The rules governing the joining of the circles apply to the diph thong ī. In the words *Nile*, *tile*, for instance, the sign is placed outside the angle, as is done in *nail*, *tale*.

(b) In some words it will be found unnecessary to write the line through the large circle to express the diphthong. For example, it is sufficient to write *mat* for *might*, as "it mat (might) be," and *ma* for *my*, as "in ma (my) opinion," etc. Other-common examples are: *life, quite, lively.*

VOWEL COMBINATIONS

45. Consecutive vowels which do not form a pure diphthong are joined in their natural order.

Leo	l ē ō		olio	ō l ĭ ō	
Owen	ō ĕ n		cameo	k ă m ĕ ō	
Noah	n ō a		snowy	s n ō ĭ	

NOTE: When long ō is followed by a small circle, as in *Owen*, (ō ĕ n), the dash is usually placed beneath the hook.

46. Any vowel following the diphthong *i* is expressed by the small circle within the large circle.

via	v ī a		lion	l ī ŭ n	
fiat	f ī ă t		science	s ī ĕ n s	
dial	d ī a l		iota	ī ō t a	

NOTE: When *io* begins a word it is written (as in *iota*, given above) with the same movement as *o* in longhand, which it resembles in appearance.

47. Where necessary, short *i* followed by *a* as in *mania*, is expressed by the large circle with a *dot* placed within it; and *e* followed by any large circle vowel sound by the large circle with a *dash* within it. These distinctions are seldom necessary.

mania	m ā n ĭ a		Olympia	o l ĭ m p ĭ a	
medial	m ē d ĭ a l		ammonia	ă m ō n ĭ a	
create	k r ē ā t		Lydia	l ĭ d ĭ a	

48. There are a few words in which there are no consonants. In such words the dot for the aspirate, or the marks distinguishing the vowel sounds, should be used.

ah!		who		ye	
awe		hue, hew		yea	
owe, oh!		hay		woe	
hoe		high		woo	

WORD-SIGNS AND PHRASES

allow	point, appoint	I find	
behind	right, write	wire	
find	side	please wire	
how, out	use	please write	
kind	usual-ly, wish	write me	
light	while	your kind letter	
like	why	on this side	
new	wife	I would like	

SPECIAL BUSINESS PHRASES

Dear Sir   Yours truly   Yours very truly

Dear Madam   Very truly yours   Yours respectfully

READING EXERCISE

WRITING EXERCISE

1. Julia Marlowe will-not play Ophelia this year.
2. If-you-find that Mr. Boyd is out of-the city, please-wire-me so that I-can get other help for you.
3. Please-write-me fully as-to what you do about increasing the price on-the lots in Butte.
4. Before we publish the book we-must find out about the size of type which you-wish us to use.
5. The chimes will ring in the new year

SEVENTH LESSON

BLENDED CONSONANTS

49. When two straight lines form an obtuse or blunt angle, the natural tendency of the hand is to "slur" the angle and allow the lines to form a curve, thus:

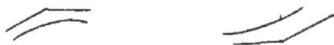

The characters have been so arranged that many frequent combinations form an obtuse angle, and this angle not being observed, the lines blend naturally in the form of a curve.

50. All of the following blended consonants are written upwards from the line of writing:

TEN, DEN	*as in* tenor	denote	
TEM, DEM	*as in* temper	demolish	
ENT, END	*as in* paint	bond	
EMT, EMD	*as in* prompt	deemed	

NOTES: (a) As the combinations are pronounced as syllables, minor vowels occurring between the consonants are omitted, but diphthongs and strongly accented vowels are inserted. For instance, *dean, dine, team, tame, dome, dime,* are written in full. The blend is used, however, in words ending in *tain* as *detain*

(b) Although the blends *ent, end, emt, emd* are pronounced as syllables, just as *sh* is pronounced *ish,* the vowel preceding the blend is seldom omitted, except at the beginning of a word, as in *entry, entail.*

39

GENERAL EXERCISE

tenets		detain		temple	
tenant		threaten		attempt	
tenacious (a)		tendency		demur	
dense		attendance		wisdom	
condense		timid		entry	
condensation		freedom		entail	
continent		kingdom		plenty	
condemn		contempla-tion		moaned	
intention (b)		anatomy		dawned	
extension		phantom		fastened	
contention		autumn		lamed	
sweeten		sanctum		seemed	
latent (b)		brand		steamed	
mutiny		lined		exempt	
stencil		signed		shamed	
mutton		faint		Indian	
obtain		gained		addenda (b)	

NOTES: (a) The rule given in Paragraph 16 applies to the circle between the blended consonants and straight lines as in the word *tenacious*

(b) Where it is possible to use either *ten, den,* or *ent, end,* the *ten, den* blend is given the preference.

51. In joining *d* to *f* or *v*, and *j* to *ent*, *end*, the angle is obscured in rapid writing, and the combination is written with one impulse of the pen.

DEF-V, TIVE *as in* defeat native

JENT-D, PENT-D *as in* gentle happened

NOTE: It will be found that *tive* generally occurs at the end of words, as in *native*, and cannot be confused with *def*, *dev*, which generally occur at the beginning of words, as in *defame*.

GENERAL EXERCISE

defy		deficit		genteel	
edify		restive		Gentile	
edifice		festive		legend	
deface		motive		regent	
defame		attentive		*contingent*	
defense		tentative		tangent	
devout		cheapened		pageant	
divine		ripened		depend	
divide		rampant		spent	
diffidence		opened		*expend*	
devise		cogent		*im*pend*ing*	

52. The syllables *men, mem* are expressed by lengthening *m*, that is, by joining *m* and *n; ted, ded, det,* by a long stroke upwards, equal to *t* and *d* joined; *ses* or *sus,* by joining the two signs for *s; xes,* by joining *x* and *s.*

MEN, MEM	———	*as in*	men*tion*	memory	
TED, DED, DET		*as in*	heated	seated	
SES		*as in*	passes	faces	
XES		*as in*	boxes	mixes	

NOTES: The combination *det* usually occurs at the beginning of words, as in *detach, detest,* while *ded, ted,* usually occur at the end of words.

The stroke is used to express *ted, ded* after short words only, a disjoined dash being more convenient in most words as explained in Par. 53.

GENERAL EXERCISE

man	effeminate	Roman
many	nominate	romance
menace	examine	Ottoman
minute	maintain	famine
month	minimum	human
amen	stamina	Manhattan
acumen	women	common*ly*
immense	omen	detach
emanate	ominous	detec*tion*
memoir	remain	waited

masses	‒ℐ	teases	↗	sustain	↝
guesses	⌒	possess	↗	cessation	⤳
races	⌒	leases	‿ℐ	annexes	⌐ℐ
basis	ᔑ	fences	↙	taxes	↗

NOTE: In rapid writing the first *s* in *ses* may become obscure, and yet the second *s*, being written contrary to the rule for writing a single *s*, clearly indicates the plural form. Compare *face, faces, case, cases, pass, passes*.

53. At the end of many words *ted*, *ded*, and sometimes *ed*, may be expressed by *t* placed beneath or close to the preceding character.

invited ⌐ divided ⌒ demanded ⌒ printed ⌒

54. Advantage may be taken of the blending principle in phrase writing, thus: *t-me* for *to me*, *t-do* for *to do*.

to-day	⟋	to meet	⌒	ought to know	⌒
to do	⟋	to make	⌒	at any time	⌒
to draw	⟋	to my	⌒	what to do	⌒
to mean	⌒	to know	⌒	in due time	⌒

WORD-SIGNS AND PHRASES

and, end	⌣	assist	↗	date, did	⟋
hand	⌣	attention	⌒	definite	↻
agent	⟋	between	⌒	devote	↻

differ-ent/ence	⟋	society	⟨	and I am	⟋
difficult-y	⟨	time	⟋	at hand	⟍
duty	⟋	to-morrow	⟋	all my time	⟋
endure	⟋	want	⟋	at that time	⟋
exist-ence	⟩	went	⟋	for the time	⟋
gentlemen	⟃	in time	⟋	your attention	⟋
Messrs.	⟋	and there	⟋	kind attention	⟋
says, system	⟋	and there is	⟋	every attention	⟋
season	⟋	and am	⟋	my attention	⟋

READING EXERCISE

WRITING EXERCISE

1. The society asks for different working conditions and a minimum wage law.

2. The memoirs of-this famous man read like a romance; such a book will-be an inspiration to-me.

3. Andrew Temple will study printing and book binding in the evening classes at the Manhattan Academy.

4. Your-letter reached me, but I-have had no time to-make the definite reply demanded.

5. That you-are in business means that you-are doing something for-which mankind is willing to-give you money.

6. We-can-not grant the extension of-time you-wish, and if-the money does-not reach us by-the date mentioned, we-shall draw on-you through our bank.

7. The auditor who was sent to examine the books for-the season had to devote a month to-the work.

EIGHTH LESSON

---

55. The circle or loop is written with a reverse movement to express R:

(a) Before or after straight lines, or between two straight lines in the same direction.

Before		*After*		*Between*	
art		tar		tart	
arm		mar		marmot	
harsh		share		tardy	

(b) Between a horizontal and an upward character.

mart	cart	lard	garden

(c) Between a downward character and T, D, N, M.

pert	barn	chart	farm

NOTE: As there is a tendency in rapid writing to curve a straight line when it is followed by a circle, the distinctive method of joining the circle when reversed after Ch, J, illustrated in *chart* (compare with *pert*), is adopted to prevent any possibility of misreading.

46

(d) Between SH, CH, J, and L.

churl   Charles   charlatan   Jarley

56. By changing the form of the reversed circle to a *loop* at the end of a straight line, the letter S is added·

dares   manners   stars   tires

readers   preachers   cheers   ledgers

57. Before straight lines S in *ser*, *cer*, *sar*, and Th in *ther*, *thir*, may be written contrary to the usual method of joining to express R.

sermon   assert   serge   sardine

concern   concert   exert   insert

desert   third   thirty   Thermos

GENERAL EXERCISE

heart	army	harness
hearty	hard	Armenia
heartily	harm	earn

yearn		oyster		guarantee	
yard		barter		courtesy	
Yarmouth		dirty		Hibbard	
harmony		Tartar		pardon	
Armada		tender		bird	
arch		cashier		burden	
hermit		mermaid		spared	
hurt*		murmur		shepherd	
urge*		murder		shirt	
near		martyr		charter	
mere		marten		journey	
jeer		girder		sojourn	
dear		alert		adjourn	
domineer		billiard		germ	
anger		Hilliard		Charlotte	
tire		poniard		hammers	
attire		card		farmers	
dart		carter		soldiers	
mutter		cartridge		surname	

*It is generally more facile to use the circle for the obscure vowel sound heard in *ur*.

58. The letter R is omitted without reversing:

(a) In many words containing *ar, er:*

starch		cargo		perverse	
large		clergy		perversity	
margin		certain		learn	
alarm		serve		term	
tarnish		surface		turn	
argue		surprise		lantern	
starva- tion		surplus		northern	
gargle		traverse		southern	

(b) In many words containing *or:*

ordain	ornate	sort	retort
extort	indorse	border	absorb

(c) In words beginning with *war, wor:*

war	warn	ward	worse

59. The reversing principle is used to express **L** in the following words:

till, teil	deal	mail	mile

smile	still	style	detail

NOTE: The plural of these words is expressed by a reversed *loop* — see Par. 56.

deals	mails	styles	details

WORD-SIGNS

certificate	merchandise	particular
determine	order	territory
firm	organize- organization	trust
first	question	until
merchant	refer-ence	word

READING EXERCISE

WRITING EXERCISE

1. The poems of Robert Burns portray his love for mankind as shown in-the line "A man's a man for all that."

2. We-can-not fill your first order until we-have heard from-your references.

3. In-the northern territory this organization sells only to certain firms, but in-the southern cities it does a large mail order business.

4. The firm in-question deals in hardware and sells all styles of churns, hammers and other tools to-the farmers in-this and bordering counties.

NINTH LESSON

WORD-SIGNS

60. The forms on this page should be transcribed without referring to the key. Afterwards the student should compare his transcript with the key, and make corrections.

REVIEW EXERCISE ON WORD-SIGNS

KEY TO REVIEW EXERCISE ON WORD-SIGNS

61. The student should test his knowledge of the word-signs by writing the following words in shorthand, afterwards comparing the forms he has written with those given on the opposite page. In doing this it is a good plan to place a ring around any word incorrectly written, and afterwards write several lines of the correct form.

1. a-an, about, above, after, agent, all, allow, am-more, and-end, any, are-our, ask, assist.

2. at-it, attention, be-but-by, become-book, been-bound, before-behalf, behind, belief-believe, between, beyond, body, business, call, can.

3. care, cause-because, certificate, change-which, check, company-keep, could, course, date-did, definite, desire, determine.

4. devote, differ-ent-ence, difficult-y, duty, else-list, endure, ever-y, exist-ence, fall-follow, far-favor, find, firm, first.

5. for, form-from, friend-ly, full-y, gave, gentlemen, give-n, glad, go-good, great, hand.

6. have, he, how-out, I, in-not, inclose, instant-instance, is-his, judge, kind, let-letter, light, like.

7. little, long, look, market-Mr., Messrs., most, move, much, must.

8. name, new, next, of, one, order, organize-organization, other, particular, please, point-appoint, public-publish, put.

9. question, real-regard, receive, refer-ence, reply, represent, right-write, says-system, season, shall-ship, should, side, society, some.

10. soon, speak-speech, state, such, sure-ly, teach, territory, than-then, that, the, their-there, them, they, thing-think, this, those.

11. time, told, to-morrow, trust, until, upon, use, usual-ly-wish, very, want, was, week, well-will, went.

12. were, what, when, where, while, why, wife, wire, word, work, world, would, yes, you-your.

LIST OF ADDITIONAL WORD-SIGNS

62. Many of these words are written in accordance with rules given at a later stage of the study, but are presented now so that the student may begin dictation on connected matter. As these words are of frequent occurrence, the forms should be diligently practiced, in order to gain facility in writing them.

accept-ance		bring	
accord		capital	
accordance		car, correct	
acknowledge		carry	
acquaint-ance		character	
advantage		charge	
advertise		clear-ly	
again		clerk	
agree		collect	
always		consider-ation	
arrange-ment		copy	
avoid		corporation	
beauty		correspond-ence	
better		cover	
bill		credit	

custom		import-ant/ance	
deliver		improve-ment	
direct		industry	
dollar		influence	
draft		insur-e/ance	
duplicate		invoice	
during, Dr.		jury	
educate		mortgage	
effect		never	
either		newspaper	
enough		object	
experience		oblige	
fault (see *fall*)		occasion	
future		occup-y/ation	
God		office	
gone		official	
got		opinion	
govern-ment		part	
house		princip-al/le	
immediate-ly		publication	

pupil		spirit	
quality		stand	
quantity		stock	
railroad		strange	
railway		strong, strength	
recent		suggest-ion	
record		thank	
regret		thorough-ly, three	
remark		throughout	
remit-tance		truth	
report		typewriter	
respect-ful-ly		value	
return		vowel	
satis-$^{fy}_{factory}$		wealth (see *well*)	
satisfaction		with	
send		without	
signific-$^{ant}_{ance}$		wonder	
sir		yesterday	
small		young	

NOTES: (a) The plural of word-signs ending in *S* is formed as follows.

causes	instances	respects

(b) To express the plural of word-signs ending in a circle and of some words ending in a loop, a slight change is made in the manner of joining S.

names	cares	carries

families	homilies	anomalies

(c) After a circle vowel, *ly* is written outside the preceding consonant, thus

namely	dearly	likely

daily	nearly	merely

(d) *Ly* is added to words ending in the diphthong *i* by the double circle

lightly	kindly	rightly

READING EXERCISE

WRITING EXERCISE

1. The government will insure the goods against loss.

2. Your acceptance of our order is in accordance with the arrangement, a copy of which I gave to your clerk.

3. His long experience in writing advertising copy will be an advantage to the new official in his work with the insurance corporation.

4. Quality is more important than quantity. Your motto should be "Not how much, but how well."

5. The charge of the judge will oblige the jury to consider the character and occupation of the victim.

6. The agent reports that he could not send the book yesterday but that he will deliver it to-morrow without fail.

7. The typewriter is of great value in the business office. In truth it is difficult to do business without one.

8. He says that most of his pupils wish to take the full course and that he is planning the organization of a new class at the beginning of next month.

9. We suggest that the society arrange to take some action on this report and that such action be made a part of the record.

10. Please send a check with your next order or we cannot accord it immediate attention.

11. The report of this season's business is thoroughly satisfactory.

12. The object of this publication is to place before the public the truth about the recent report on the railway stock.

TENTH LESSON

COMPOUND WORDS

63. A number of compounds may be obtained by joining simple word-signs, as illustrated in the second lesson by the word "before." The following words are formed on the same principle:

any:

be:

ever-y:

here:

there:

where:

soever:

some:

with:

NOTE: Slight modifications or omissions are made in the forms for *anywhere*, *anyhow*, *hereinafter*, *herewith*, *however*, *sometime*, and *somewhere*. These should receive special attention. The form for *notwithstanding* is *not-with-s*.

MISCELLANEOUS COMPOUNDS

nobody		nevertheless		otherwise	
meanwhile		standpoint		thanksgiving	

KEY TO COMPOUND WORDS

any: anybody, anyone, anywhere, anyhow.

be: before, beforehand, behindhand, belong, beside.

ever-y: whatever, whenever, whichever, however, whoever, everybody, everyone, everywhere.

here: hereafter, herein, hereinafter, hereinbefore, hereon, hereto, heretofore, hereunto, herewith.

there: thereafter, therein, therefore, therefrom, thereon, thereto, thereupon, therewith.

where: whereabouts, whereas, wherever, wherefore, wherein, whereof, whereon, elsewhere.

soever: whatsoever, wheresoever, whensoever, whosoever, whomsoever.

some: somebody, somehow, someone, sometime, somewhat, somewhere.

with: within, withstand, forthwith, notwithstanding.

DERIVATIVES, ETC.

64. After abbreviated words and words ending in a reversed circle, a short dash struck upward is used to express the past tense; the disjoined *r* expresses the terminations *er, or,* and the disjoined *ri,* expresses *ary, ory.*

wanted		director		caller	
experienced		directory		customary	
dearer		nearer		murderer	

NOTE: When the forms are distinctive, *er, or, ary, ory*, may be joined, as in *greater, boundary, receiver, stronger, writer, reporter*.

65. When a word-sign ends with the *last consonant of the word*, the reversing principle may be used to express *er* after straight lines.

| sooner | longer | firmer | teacher |

66. The word-signs *after* (*af*) and *out* (*ow*) may be used as prefix forms.

| aftertimes | afternoon | outstanding | outside |

GENERAL EXERCISE

cared		collected		creditor	
favored		corrected		fuller	
returned		insured		giver	
believed		insurer		kinder	
caused		advertiser		recorder	
inclosed		clearer		speaker	

sender		thinker		afterglow	
shipper		worker		outgoing	
publisher		afterthought		outfit	

THE ABBREVIATING PRINCIPLE

67. Many long words may be abbreviated by dropping the terminations.   It would be a waste of time and effort to write more of a word than is necessary to suggest it when transcribing.   This principle is already familiar in longhand, as *Rev.* for *Reverend, ans.* for *answer, Jan.* for *January, Phila.* for *Philadelphia,* etc.

The extent to which the principle may be applied depends upon the familiarity of the writer with the words and subject matter.   Every writer can apply it easily and naturally to familiar words, and adapt it to the special requirements of the line of work in which he may be engaged.

The words given in this lesson are among the most common and useful illustrations of the application of this principle.   When these have been studied, it will be easy to apply the principle in general practice.   Many of the words given in subsequent lessons are abbreviated in this way.   It is important to bear in mind that all the words so abbreviated will usually occur in sentences. For instance in the sentence "He was received with great enthusiasm," it would be sufficient to write *enthus* for *enthusiasm;* and the same form might be used for *enthusiastic* in "He met with a most enthusiastic reception."

ILLUSTRATION OF ABBREVIATING PRINCIPLE

It is *pos*sible that the *suc*cess of the *maga*zine may

make it *neces*sary to change the *pol*icy of the *asso*ciation

at the next meeting in *Phila*delphia sometime in *Jan*uary.

Have you a *memo*randum of their *finan*cial standing?

We cannot *can*cel the *bal*ance. The *Feb*ruary *num*ber will

contain an *orig*inal story by a very *promin*ent writer.

Please *an*swer this letter before *Sep*tember first. We

*remem*ber your *co-op*eration at that time and we shall show

our *appre*ciation when there is an *oppor*tunity to do so.

Exercise on Abbreviating Principle

The following words are to be written in shorthand, and afterwards compared with the forms given on the opposite page:

1. aband(on), abbrev(iate), abs(ent), abso(lute), accus(tom), alph(abet), ambass(ador), anim(al), anon(ymous), ans(wer).

2. apol(ogize), apprec(iate), assoc(iation), attit(ude), attrib(ute), bal(ance), brill(iant), cal(culate), canc(el).

3. cap(able), Cath(olic), celeb(rate), chil(dren), collat(eral), conseq(uence), co-op(erate), deg(ree).

4. delib(erate), demons(tiate), dict(ate), dilap(idate), dilig(ence), dis(count), eloq(uent), emin(ent).

5 Eng(land), enthus(iasm), entit(le), estab(lish), estim(ate), fam(iliar), finan(cial), freq(uent), gen(eral).

6. grat(itude), hund(red), inaug(urate), indic(ate), innoc(ence), invol(ve), irresis(tible), journ(al).

7. knowl(edge), lang(uage), leg(al), leng(th), lib(erty), loc(al), mag(azine).

8. mat(ter), melan(choly), memo(randum), mod(erate), neg(lect), negoti(ate), num(ber).

9. num(erous), obse(rve), obv(ious), oppor(tunity), ordin(ary), orig(inal), pamph(let), pecu(liar), pecun(iary), perman(ent).

10 perpend(icular), pleas(ant), pol(icy), pop(ular), pos(sible), pov(erty), predeces(sor), pref(er), prej(udice), prelim(inary)

11. prep(are), pres(ent), presi(de), priv(ilege), promin(ent), rath(er), relinq(uish), remem(ber).

12. remons(trate), rev(erend), ridic(ulous), scrup(ulous), separ(ate), sev(eral), simil(ar), simul(taneous), singu(lar)

13. splend(id), suc(cess), suf(ficient), synon(ymous), temp(erance), trav(el), unan(imous), un(ion), vul(gar)

EXERCISE ON ABBREVIATING PRINCIPLE

The following words are to be transcribed without referring to the key on the opposite page until the work has been completed.

1.
2.
3.
4.
5.
6.
7.
8.
9.
10.
11.
12.
13.

68. The Abbreviating Principle may be applied to a *short* word when a distinctive outline is secured.   Usually this is done after a diphthong or strongly sounded vowel, as illustrated in the word-signs *right-write, find, light, side.* The following are useful examples:

bright		client		trade	
delight		private		grade	
arrive		trial		freight	
derive		doubt		claim	
decide		loyal-ty		poor	
unite		power		cure	
strike		proud		night	
entire		thousand		to-night	

Days and Months

Sunday		January		August	
Monday		February		September	
Tuesday		March		October	
Wednesday		April		November	
Thursday		May		December	
Friday		June			
Saturday		July			

FIGURES, ETC.

69. After numerals the word *dollars* is expressed by *d;* *hundred* by *n* placed under the numeral; *thousand* by *th;* *million* by *m* placed on the line close to the numeral; *billion* by *b;* *pounds* (weight or money) by *p;* *gallons* by *g;* *barrels* by *br;* *bushels* by *bsh;* *feet* by *f;* *francs* by *fr;* *cwt* by *nw;* *o'clock* by *o* placed over the numeral:

$5		£5,000	
500		£500,000	
$500		five gallons	
5,000		five barrels	
$5,000		five bushels	
500,000		five feet	
5,000,000		five cwt.	
$5,000,000		five o'clock	
5 lbs. (or £5)		500 feet	
500 lbs. (or £500)		five francs	

70. These signs may be used after the article *a* and such words as *per, few, several:*

a dollar		few thousand dollars	
a thousand dollars		a pound	

a hundred thousand		per hundred	⊆
several hundred		a million	· ——
several hundred dollars		a gallon	

71. *Cents* when preceded by dollars may be expressed by writing the figures representing them very small and above the numerals for the dollars; when not preceded by dollars the sign for *s* is placed above the figures. *Per cent* is expressed by *s* written below the figures; *per cent per annum* by adding *n* to per cent.

$8.50   five cents   five per cent   five per cent per annum

READING EXERCISE

[shorthand notation]

WRITING EXERCISE

1. Elsewhere in this issue you will find a notice which should be read by everyone who desires general knowledge about the legal rights of women in the different states in the union.

2. He advertised in the afternoon papers for an experienced collector and by 10 o'clock that night a hundred replies were received.

3. The eloquent speaker was greeted with enthusiastic applause which indicated that his views were popular.

4. If the quality of this merchandise is not as represented you may return the goods to us and we will give you credit for them, but we cannot possibly allow you any discount on the balance.

5. The creditor will not relinquish the claim which his first mortgage gives him, and therefore we cannot sell the entire stock at auction as the other creditors suggested.

6. We allow a discount of 5% on cash sales.

7. Some customers take advantage of this even when they find it necessary to borrow the money.

ELEVENTH LESSON

PHRASE-WRITING

72. The student should cultivate the practice of joining small words, for without it great proficiency can never be attained. All the common phrases consisting of two or three words should be written with the same facility as an ordinary word-form, but nothing is gained by straining after special forms for uncommon phrases, or where the outline requires more than five efforts of the pen. While experience must ever be the supreme teacher in phrase-writing, the following suggestions will be useful.

(*a*) At the outset short and common words only should be joined.

(*b*) The words should make good sense if standing alone, as *I am glad.*

(*c*) The outlines for the words should be capable of being easily joined.

(*d*) Phrases that carry the hand away from the line of writing should be avoided; in other words, the writer should aim at onward movement.

(*e*) Pronouns are generally joined to the words they precede, as *I am, I shall, you can, we have.*

(*f*) A qualifying word may be joined to the word it qualifies, as *good men.*

(*g*) The prepositions *to, of, in* and *with,* and the conjunction *and*

70

are generally joined to the words they precede, as *to have, of which, in case, with this, and there.*

(*h*) The auxiliary verbs *should, would, could* are generally joined to the words they precede, as *should be, would be, could be.*

In practicing the phrases given in this manual, the student should keep steadily in mind that they are given as *examples*, and that he is to form his own phrases on similar lines in general practice. He should study the phrases here given with a view of noting not only the nature of the joinings, but also the nature of the words that are joined.

GENERAL EXERCISE

it is		of our		I am	
of the		of all		I can	
to the		we are		I have	
to this		from the		you have	
in the		from you		I would	
on the		which the		I will	
of his		which is		you can	
of their		which can		you will	
of your		that the		of which	
is the		there is		it was	
in our		there are		in which	

by the		all right		in this	
by which		there were		in these	
to you		there will		in those	
for the		may be		in thus	
for this		will be		I inclose	
with the		would be		we inclose	
with this		at hand		in regard	

Word Modifications

Very useful and distinctive phrase-forms are obtained by modifying the forms for certain words.

73. Before words beginning with a downward character or O, R, L, *to* is expressed by *t*.

to be		to favor		to honor	
to have		to please		to receive	
to pay		to believe		to look	

74. When repeated in a phrase, the word *as* is expressed by *s:*

as well as		as great as		as many as	
as good as		as much as		as long as	

75. In phrases *been* is expressed by *b:*

have been   has been   it has been

I have been   had been   I have not been

76. After *be* or *been* the word *able* is expressed by *a:*

to be able   shall be able

have been able   has not been able

would be able   will be able

should be able   have not been able

77. The following method of expressing *had* after nouns should be carefully noted:

I had   they had   we had   you had

78. When *do not* is preceded by a pronoun, it is expressed by the sign for *dn.*

I do not   we do not

you do not   I do not think

they do not   you do not know

79. *Don't* is distinguished from *do not* by writing *dōn.*

I don't think   you don't know   I don't believe

80. The phrase *was not* may be easily and legibly expressed by writing *wasn't*, that is, by joining *s* to *nt* without an angle. For the same reason, *it is not* is written *it isn't* and *there is not* is written *there isn't*. If the contractions *wasn't, isn't* need to be clearly indicated, an apostrophe is placed over the forms.

it is not	it was not	he was not	it wasn't

81. The words *ago, early, few, him, hope, sorry, want,* are modified as shown in the following phrase-forms:

weeks *ago*		to *him*	
months ago		I told him	
years ago		we told him	
at an *early* date		I *hope*	
at an early day		we hope	
early reply		I am *sorry*	
few days		we are sorry	
few days ago		I *want*	
few months		you want	
few months ago		we want	
few minutes		if you want	
few minutes ago		do you want	

OMISSION OF WORDS

82. The phrase *of the* may be omitted and its omission implied by writing the words it connects close together.

Your letter of the 4th inst.   time of the day

end of the week   state of the market

credit of the firm   list of the people

83. The words *from* and *to* are omitted in such phrases as *from time to time*.

from time to time   from month to month

from day to day   from year to year

from week to week   from season to season

84. The word *after* is omitted in such phrases as *day after day*, but the words are not joined.

time after time   week after week

day after day   month after month

hour after hour   year after year

85. The word *by* is omitted in such phrases as *day by day*, the last word being written a little below the first word.

day by day   line by line

week by week   little by little

86. The word *to* is omitted after the words *able, according, glad, like, order, please, reference, regard, regret, relative, respect, wish.*

able to say		in reference to the matter	
in respect to the		glad to see	
in regard to the matter		I regret to say	
in reference to the		wish to say	

87. Any unimportant word may be omitted where the grammatical construction of the sentence would compel its restoration when transcribing.

in the world		some of them	
here and there		week or two	
more and more		son-in-law	

GENERAL EXERCISE

to see		*as* near *as*	
to ship		as low as	
to which		as soon as	
to reach		you have *been*	
to like		there has been	
to represent		what has been	
to sell		had been *able*	

will not be able		day or two	
have you not been able		in a day or two	
I *had* been		in reply to your	
they had been		ought to receive	
I *do not* see		out of the question	
I do not know		in a week or two	
we do not know		to-day or to-morrow	
I do not like		some of those	
I *don't* see		by the way	
there *was not*		hand in hand	
days *ago*		that is to say	
ten days ago		system of government	
for a *few* days		form of government	
I *hope* to hear		one of our	
I am *sorry* to say		one or two	
if you *want* any		one of the best	
particulars *of the* work		ought to be	
cheer *after* cheer		ought to have	
side *by* side		more or less	
on the question		one of the most	

SPECIAL BUSINESS PHRASES
(See Also Page 37)

Dear Sirs		Very respectfully	
Dear Mr.		Cordially yours	
My dear Sir		Very cordially yours	
Yours sincerely		I am in receipt	
Yours very sin-cerely		We are in receipt	
Very sincerely		I am in receipt of your favor	
Very sincerely yours		We are in receipt of your favor	
Sincerely yours		I am in receipt of your letter	

READING EXERCISE

WRITING EXERCISE

1

Dear Madam:

We learn from your letter of May 10 that you are returning the books which we sent you a few months ago. You will be credited with these books when they reach us and the charge for them will be canceled. We are glad to know that you appreciate our courtesy in accepting their return. When you need anything more in)ur line, you will find us ever ready to serve yo**.

Very sincerely yours, (77)

2

Dear Sir:

We have your recent letter asking us to take advertising space in your newspaper. Our advertising plans for the next few months will not allow us to take any more newspaper space at this time. If you will bring this matter to our attention again in about three months, we may be able to arrange for a full page in the holiday issue to which you refer.

Very cordially yours, (72)
140

TWELFTH LESSON

OMISSION OF VOWELS

88. When two vowels not forming a pure diphthong come together, the minor or unaccented vowel may be omitted, and for convenience in writing many words the circle may be omitted in the diphthong *u*.

deity	ratio	royal	radius

due	tune	music	continue

89. In the body of a word short *u* and *ow* are omitted before *n, m, ng, nk, nt, nd*.

run	come	sun	round

found	rung	sunk	pungent

NOTES: (a) The short *u* is not omitted when it occurs between two horizontal straight strokes, as in *nun, numb*.

(b) The omission of *ow* between two horizontal straight strokes is indicated by the "jog" or broken line, as in *renown, announce*.

80

90. The vowel is omitted in the prefixes *be*, *de*, *re*, *dis*, *mis*.

beneath	depend	revise	distance

misgivings	begun	debar	disease

NOTES: (a) The vowel is retained when *de* precedes K, G, as in *decay, degrade*.
(b) The vowel is retained when *re* precedes the forward characters, K, G, R, L, N, M, T, D, as in *recast, regain, rewrite, relate, renown, remiss, retail, redound*

91. The vowel is omitted in *per*, *pur*, *pro*, and in the termination *age*.

permit	pursuit	profound	profess

manage	message	cartage	bondage

NOTE: When *pro* occurs before an upward character or *K* — as in *protest, procrastinate*—it is more convenient to insert the vowel; when *per* occurs before an upward character — as in *perturb, pertain, perdition* — the reversing principle expresses R.

92. The vowels *ŭ*, *ōo* are omitted after R or L when followed by Sh, Ch, J.

rush	flush	solution	drudge

93. The vowel is omitted in the terminations *tition, tation, dition, dation, nition, nation, mission, mation.*

repetition	addition	ignition	omission

station	gradation	stagnation	formation

GENERAL PRINCIPLES

94. While the omission of vowels in general is left to a very large extent to the judgment of the writer, the following suggestions will be of assistance:

(*a*) A vowel is often omitted between two reverse curves.

maker	struck	skill	scarce

attract	eager	secure	gulf

(*b*) A hook vowel is often omitted between T, D, R, L, and P, B.

stop	drop	Dublin	adoption

(*c*) A circle vowel is often omitted between P, B, and a horizontal or upward character.

pity	rapid	open	bad

OMISSION OF CONSONANTS

95. D is omitted when it immediately precedes M or V.

admit	administer	adverb	advocate

NOTE: In the words *admire, advise, advance*, coming under this rule, the initial vowel may be omitted. This enables the writer to form such useful phrases as *I admire, we admire, to advise, I advise, we advise, to advance, in advance.*

96. When slightly enunciated, T or D is omitted at the end of a word.

fact	best	detect	mind

defect	insist	resist	desist

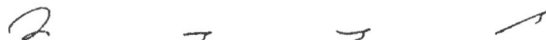

97. The combination *ld* is expressed by raising the end of L.

old	field	killed	Arnold

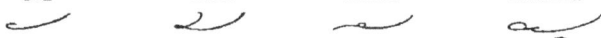

building	oewilder	golden	Reynolds

GENERAL EXERCISE

arduous	astound	deserve
genius	redound	debase
genuine	moun- tainous	debate
astute	surmount	decision
musician	renounce	discharge
virtue	announce	disarm
theory	legion	discern
museum	rejoice	distort
harmo- nious	review	discard
ceremo- nious	repent	misprint
fun	respond	misquote
lunch	replace	misguide
column	reside	perhaps
front	resort	permission
brown	resource	promotion
drown	begrudge	prolong
sound	bequeath	propel
surround	betray	provide
foundry	beseech	proper

sausage		tradition		pithy	
dotage		foundation		apathy	
passage		ammunition		carpet	
damage		fascination		homeopathy	
baggage		nomination		happen	
package		assassination		facile	
average		determination		normal	
crush		domination		formal	
blush		animation		vernal	
resolution		estimation		mental	
dissolution		occur		dental	
visitation		currency		mortal	
citation		sugar		actual	
dictation		career		mutual	
agitation		massacre		habitual	
ostentation		equal		perpetual	
hesitation		accuracy		amateur	
recitation		carbon		torture	
imitation		augur		picture	
edition		epithet		creature	

feature	extenuation	evident
venture	attest	exact
event	attestation	contact
eventual	detest	consist
adventure	detestation	persist
failure	past	demand
error	hardest	bold
serious	deduct	child
previous	resident	Leopold
tuition	president	folder

98. The following words coming under the rules given in this lesson are also useful illustrations of the Abbreviating Principle.

benefit	disturb	probable
discuss	manufacture	progress
distinct	misfortune	punctual
distinguish	mistake	purchase
disagree-ment	perfect	purpose
disappoint-ment	person-al	respons-$^{e}_{ible}$

NOTE: In *disagree, disappoint* and their derivatives, it is found convenient to write *d* for *dis*.

READING EXERCISE

WRITING EXERCISE

1. The theory was advanced that a solution of the bewildering mystery could be found only by following up every clue.

2. A special meeting was announced for the purpose of discussing the formation of a society for the benefit of the metal workers in the foundry.

3. Much damage was done to the baggage through rough handling and one package was entirely crushed.

4. Silence about the details of your office work is a virtue. The repetition of an innocent remark has often caused the failure of an important business deal.

5. The manager soon found there were profound misgivings about the outcome of the expedition.

THIRTEENTH LESSON

99. Most of the joined prefixes are already familiar to the student. They are repeated at this time for the purpose of furnishing sufficient practice to eliminate hesitation in using them in actual work.

100. Al, expressed by *aw*; and **Ul,** by *u*.

almost	also	ultimo (ult.)	ulcer

101. Com, Con, Coun, Cog, expressed by *k*.

competition	confess	counsel	cognomen

NOTES: (a) Before *t* or *d* the prefix form may express *can*.

cantaloupe	candidate	candor	candle

(b) When Com or Con is followed by a vowel or by *r* or *l*, write *km* for *com* and *kn* for *con*.

comedy	comrade	conic	Conroy

88

102. Em, Im, expressed by *m*; and En, In, Un, by *n*.

embers	imprint	enjoin	unjust

103. (*a*) The prefix forms for *em, im, en, in, un* are used only when a consonant follows the prefix.   When a vowel follows *em, im, en, in, un,* the initial vowel is written.

emit	innate	inner	inept

enact	unequal	imagine	inaccessible

(*b*) Negative words beginning with *im, un* are distinguished from the positive forms by the insertion of the initial vowel.

Positive

mortal	modest	known	necessary

Negative

immortal	immodest	unknown	unnecessary

104. Ex, expressed by *es*; Aux and Ox, by *os*.

exceed	expel	auxiliary	oxygen

105. For, Fore, Fur, expressed by *f*.

forgive   foresight   furnish   forearm

NOTE: When For or Fore is followed by a vowel, disjoin *f* and write the next character close to it, as in *forearm*. When *For* or *Fore* is followed by *r* or *l*, form an angle after *f*, as in *forerunner, furlong*, page 92.

106. Sub, expressed by *s*.

subdue   subpoena   submit   substance

NOTES: (a) Before R, L, Ch, J, or a hook, *s* is written contrary to rule to express *sub*.

sublime   subjoin   subway   subordinate

(b) When Sub is followed by a circle vowel, *s* is disjoined and the next character is written close to it.

subeditor   subagent   subhead   subequal

GENERAL EXERCISE

almanac		ulster	
although		compel	
ulterior		common	
ultimate		comprehend	
ultimatum		combine	

commence		cônvene	
commission		consul	
commotion		conscious	
commutation		cognate	
comity		embrace	
comatose		emperor	
conceit		impartial	
contest		imperfect	
concur		impossible	
concussion		impulse	
conditionally		impoverish	
confirm		impression	
consign		engine	
confound		encourage	
consolation		ensign	
consolidation		enchant	
consternation		infirm	
conduce		invent	
consummate		invest	
convince		investigate	

unkind		fortune	
uncouth		forsake	
unlearned		foreground	
emerge		forerunner	
emotion		furlong	
inhabit		forenoon	
immersion		furnace	
inaction		further	
uneasy		furthermore	
unnoticed		furthermost	
expert		furtive	
excess		furniture	
exaggerate		forehead	
excite		foreordain	
excursion		subside	
exhaust		subsequent	
explosion		sublease	
exhibit		suburb	
oxalic		subsist	
oxidize		subacid	

COMPOUND JOINED PREFIXES

107. Two or more simple prefixes may be joined to form compounds. A few compounds may be formed by joining *re*, *dis*, *mis*, or *non* to the prefix forms:

incontestable		inexpedient*	
unconquerable		inexplicable*	
unaccounted*		excommunicate	
incognito		inconvenient	
incandescent		inconsistent	
unimpaired*		disconcert	
uninitiated*		discontinue	
inexpensive*		preconcerted	
insubordinate		misconduct	
inform		recompense	
conform		reconcile	
comfort		recognize	
unfortunate		recommend	
unforeseen		noncontent	
encompass		subconscious	

*The initial vowel is not required because the word begins with a compound prefix.

PREFIXAL ABBREVIATIONS

108. The following are useful abbreviations under rules given in this and in previous lessons:

accomplish		economy	
afford		effort	
already		enable*	
altogether		unable*	
command		energy	
commerce		excel-$^{\text{lent}}_{\text{lence}}$	
commercial		except	
committee		exchange	
communicat-$^{\text{e}}_{\text{ion}}$		exercise	
compare		expect	
complete		explain	
conclude		express	
conclusion		force	
confiden-$^{\text{t}}_{\text{ce}}$		indeed	
congress		independen-$^{\text{t}}_{\text{ce}}$	
connect		individual	
country		subject	

*See suffix *able*, page 109.

READING EXERCISE

[shorthand characters]

WRITING EXERCISE

1. "The world will little note nor long remember what we say here, but it can never forget what they did here."

2. It needs no prophet to tell us that those who live up to their means without any thought of a reverse in life can never attain pecuniary independence.

3. To the cost of manufacturing and shipping add the profit of the manufacturer and that of the shipper—these items make up the price paid by the ultimate purchaser.

FOURTEENTH LESSON

THE TR PRINCIPLE

109. Certain prefixes or letters are disjoined to express *tr* and a following vowel. The prefix is placed above the line and very close to the remainder of the word, which rests on the line of writing.

Contr– (or *counter*)	⌒	contract	⌐	counteract	⌐
Constr–	⌐	construct	⊃	constraint	⊃
Extr– **Excl–** (or *exter*)	ʒ	extract	ʒ	exclamation	ʒ
Intr– (or *inter, en– ter, intel*)	—	intricate	—	intellect	—
Instr–	⊤	instruct	⊤	instrument	⊤—
Retr–	⌣	retract	⌐	retrograde	⌐
Restr–	⌣	restrict	⊥	restraint	⊥
Detr–	╱	detract	╱	detriment	╱
Distr–	╱	distract	╱	distribute	╱
Electr– (or *electric*)	⌒	electric	⌐	electric car	⌐
Alter	c	altercate	c	alternative	c
Ultra	⊃	ultra-violet	⊃	ultramarine	⊃

96

Centr-		central		centralize	
Later		lateral		latter-day	
Letter, Liter		literary		literal	
Matr- (or *mater*)		matri-mony		material	
Metr-		metric		metropolis	
Nitr-		nitrate		nitrogen	
Nutr-		neutral		nutrition	
Patr- (or *pater*)		patriot		paternal	
Petr- (or *peter*)		petrol		petrify	
Austr-, ostr-		Australia		ostracism	

NOTE: This principle may be extended to *abstr-*, etc., *obstr-*, the *s* being omitted:

abstract   abstruse   obstruct   obstreperous

GENERAL EXERCISE

contraction		contravene	
control		contrivance	
contribute		counterfeit	
contradict		countermand	
contraband		construction	
contrary		extravagant	
contrast		extremely	

extradition		retrieve	
extraneous		retrospect	
extraordinary		retraction	
external		retribution	
exclude		restrain	
exclusive		restriction	
internal		deterioration	
interest		distraction	
introduce		distress	
intervene		distrust	
intelligent		electricity	
intelligence		electrician	
entertain		electrotype	
enterprise		electric light	
international		alteration	
interpret		alternation	
intersect		centrifugal	
interrupt		literature	
interview		liturgy	
instruction		letterpress	

maternal		pattern	
metropolitan		patron	
nitric		petroleum	
nutriment		Austria	
patrician		ostrich	

COMPOUND DISJOINED PREFIXES

110. Some very useful compounds are obtained by joining simple syllables, such as *un*, *in*, *dis*, *re*, *non*, to disjoined prefixes.

uncontradicted		unconstrained	
uncontrolled		inextricable	
incontrovertible		uninteresting	
unrestrained		reconstruction	
redistribution		misinterpret	
disinterested		illiterate	
uninterrupted		eccentric	
unintelligent		concentration	
unintellectual		nonintervention	
indestructible		unalterable	
immaterial		compatriot	

DERIVATIVES OF WORDS ENDING IN CT

111. In forming the derivatives of words ending in *ct*, as *contract*, it is not necessary to disjoin to express *ed*, *or*, *er*, or *ive*. The *t* is omitted in the primitive form (under the rule given in Par. 96), and also its derivatives.

contracted		restrictive	
contractor		unretracted	
contractive		detracted	
constructed		active	
constructor		effected	
constructive		effective	
instructed		affected	
instructor		defective	
instructive		detected	
extracted		detective	

READING EXERCISE

WRITING EXERCISE

1. The enterprise is international in its appeal and should be of extraordinary interest to the intelligent people of every land.

2. At the close of the interview the president countersigned the order for new electric motors to equip all the high power machines.

3. We do not interpret the contract as permitting our customers to countermand their orders.

4. The international society will not intervene to restrict the working of the new extradition laws.

5. The trust will contribute a fund for the distribution of literature on the interpretation and construction of the laws regarding restraint of trade.

FIFTEENTH LESSON

DISJOINED PREFIXES—CONTINUED

112. Aggra-e-i, expressed by loop *a*; and **Anta-e-i,** by circle *a*.

aggravate	aggregate	antagonist	antipathy

113. Incli-e-u, expressed by ĭ (small circle).

incline	inclemency	include	inclusive

114. Decla-i, expressed by *de*; and **Recla-i.** by *re*.

declare	decline	reclaim	recline

NOTE: On account of the distinctive character of the form, Decla-i may be expressed without disjoining; thus

declare	decline	declaration	declaim

115. Hydra-o, expressed by ī (diphthong ī).

hydrant	hydraulic	hydropathy	hydrophobia

102

116. Magna-e-i (or **Mc**), expressed by *m*; and **Multi,** by *mu*.

magnanimous	magnificent	McDonagh	multiform

NOTE: When a distinction is required between Mc and Mac, write the stroke double length for Mac

117. Over, expressed by *o*; and **Under,** by *u*.

overdue	overthrow	understand	underneath

118. Para, expressed by *p*; and **Post,** by *p* (on the line, close to the next character).

parasite	parallel	postman	postal

119. Self, Circu-m, expressed by *s* (to the left).

selfish	self-esteem	circulation	circumvent

120. Super, Supre, expressed by *s* ("comma S").

superlative	supreme	superficial	supervise

121. Short or **Ship,** expressed by *sh*; and **Trans,** by *t*.

shorthand	shipwreck	transaction	translation

122. Suspi, Suspe, Suscep, expressed by *ses*.

suspicion	suspense	susceptible	suspect

GENERAL EXERCISE

aggrieve		hydrogen	
aggregation		hydrocarbon	
agriculture		magnet	
aggression		magnesia	
aggressive		magnify	
antidote		McKenzie	
anticipate		MacIntosh	
antecedent		McDougall	
antediluvian		multitude	
antithesis		multiply	
declamation		overtake	
declined		overbalance	
reclined		overcharge	
inclined		overlook	
inclination		overcome	
inclusion		overestimate	

underscore		circumstance	
undertake		superabundant	
underwrite		supercilious	
undercurrent		superfine	
paramount		supremacy	
paraphrase		superfluous	
paragraph		superior	
paradise		superintend	
paragon		suppress	
parapet		superb	
postage		shortcomings	
postpone		shipshape	
post-office		suspension	
postal card		suspend	
self-evident		transfer	
self-conscious		transition	
self-sufficient		transitory	
self-improvement		transformation	
circular		transcend	
circumference		transport	

Compound Disjoined Prefixes

untransacted		untransferable	
untransparent		self-control	
untranslatable		self-contradiction	
disinclination		unsuspected	
self-interest		unsuspicious	
unselfish		unsusceptible	
unparalleled		electromagnet	

123. The words *misunderstand* and *misunderstood* are expressed by *stand* and *stood* placed under *mis*, with *mis* placed on the line of writing. This is extended to *understand* and *understood* when preceded by a pronoun, a wordsign or a short phrase form.

misunderstand		I do not understand	
misunderstood		I cannot understand	
we understood		thoroughly understood	

124. The words *extra, enter, over, under, short, alter, center, counter, construe, agree, deter,* are expressed by the prefixal forms placed over the next word.

extra discount		center rail	
enter into		counter claim	

under any		construe the	
short time		Senator Cummings	

Reading Exercise

WRITING EXERCISE

1. Self-knowledge, self-reverence, self-control, these three alone lead men to supreme power.—*Emerson.*

2. It was our understanding that Doctor MacChesney was to translate that discussion on the transplanting of magnolia trees for the next issue of the Agricultural Review.

3. The extra discount allowed on the bill for goods purchased at the regular counter was not according to the new contract in which we agree to make a special price only on sales amounting to more than $200.

4. The circulation of the magazine is over fifty thousand without taking into account the extra copies sent out as exchanges.

5. It was self-evident that coal would be recognized as a contraband of war.

6. There was a general suspicion that his antagonist was a man of great intelligence and magnetism.

7. This system of shorthand is the very antithesis of the antiquated methods, and it is easy to demonstrate that it is vastly superior to any of them because there is a superabundance of evidence in its favor.

SIXTEENTH LESSON

125. **Able, Ible, Ble,** expressed by b; and **Ple,** by p.

notable	audible	noble	ample

126. **Cribe,** expressed by kr; and **Cription,** by kr-$shun$.

describe	description	prescribe	prescription

127. **Flect, Flict,** expressed by fl; and **Flection, Fliction,** by fl-$shun$.

afflict	affliction	reflect	reflection

128. **Ful,** expressed by f; **Less,** by l; **Ment,** by m; and **Ness,** by n.

thoughtful	artless	amusement	lateness

NOTES: (a) When *ment* is preceded by a *vowel*, it is generally advisable to write the word in full.

cement	raiment	lament	foment

(b) Where the root word is abbreviated to one character, *ness* is written in full, as in the word *goodness*, which is written *g-n-e-s*. If the primitive word, although a word-sign, is more fully suggested, the suffix form is used.

fullness	littleness	gladness	friendless

(c) An angle is formed in joining *ness* where the absence of an angle would give the form of a different word.

hardness	sadness	madness	lowness

harden	sadden	madden	loan

129. **Pose,** expressed by *po*; **Position,** by *po-shun*; **Pute,** by *pu*; and **Putation,** by *pu-shun*.

impose	imposition	impute	imputation

130. **Pire,** expressed by *pī*; and **Quire,** by *kī*.

aspire	inspire	conspire	respire

acquire	inquire	require	esquire

131. **Quest,** expressed by *kes*; and **Quisite,** by *kest*.

request	conquest	requisite	exquisite

132. Self, expressed by *s*; and **Selves,** by *ses*.

himself	yourself	themselves	ourselves

133. Sult, expressed by *su;* and **Sume,** by *sm*.

result	insult	assume	resume

134. Sure, expressed by *shu;* and **Jure,** by *ju*.

assure	measure	injure	perjure

135. Tion, Sion (shun); **Tient, Cient,** by *shun-t*; and Ciency, by *shun-si*.

passion	patient	ancient	efficiency

136. Worth, expressed by *uth*; and **Worthy,** by *thi*.

Harmsworth	Ainsworth	praiseworthy	trustworthy

GENERAL EXERCISE

suitable

peaceable

horrible

salable

eatable

irritable

payable

humble

nimble		simple	
readable		transcribe	
seasonable		transcription	
admissible		inscribe	
admirable		inscription	
laudable		conflict	
assignable		confliction	
attainable		inflict	
terrible		infliction	
pliable		handful	
interminable		bashful	
tangible		useful	
formidable		watchful	
incomparable		wonderful	
endurable		successful	
traceable		aimless	
credible		fearless	
trouble		homeless	
sample		breathless	
example		thoughtless	

wireless	propose
moment	proposition
defacement	proposal
ornament	depose
augment	deposition
achievement	dispose
appointment	disposition
experiment	disposal
investment	decompose
comment	repute
bareness	reputation
rudeness	compute
fairness	computation
slowness	depute
expose	deputation
exposition	dispute
suppose	disputation
supposition	transpire
oppose	expire
opposition	myself

yourselves		conjure	
consult		efficient	
desultory		deficient	
consume		deficiency	
leisure		proficient	
treasure		proficiency	
censure		Ellsworth	
pressure		blameworthy	
adjure		noteworthy	

COMPOUND JOINED SUFFIXES

feebleness		fearlessness	
hopefulness		breathlessness	
thoughtfulness		hopelessness	
playfulness		fearlessly	
carefulness		hopelessly	
hopefully		impatiently	
thoughtfully		actionable	
playfully		fashionable	
heedlessness		missionary	
thoughtlessness		consultation	

indescribable		momentary	
measurable		supplementary	
immeasurable		elementary	
requirement		complimentary	
acquirement		trustworthiness	

READING EXERCISE

WRITING EXERCISE

1. His reading was desultory and therefore without result.

2. The achievement is so remarkable that it is almost incredible, but the truth of the report is vouched for by several reliable people.

3. After careful investigation they came to a decision that the additional loans would be too large an investment for the company to undertake with the capital at its disposal at that time.

4. The shorthand notes are legible, but the transcription is not acceptable because of the lack of neatness in the work.

5. The missionary underwent indescribable torture with a fearlessness which evoked the admiration of the savages.

6. The contribution is praiseworthy for its direct treatment of the subject, but it is not suitable for use in our publication and we are therefore returning it to you.

SEVENTEENTH LESSON

DISJOINED SUFFIXES

137. Ingly, expressed by *ly*, placed in the *ing* position; Ington, expressed by *ton*, placed in the *ing* position; Ingham, expressed by *m*, placed in the *ing* position.

knowingly	Washington	Kensington	Dillingham

138. Bility, expressed by *b*; Ification, by *f*; **Gram, Grim,** by *g*; **Mental, Mentality,** by *m*; **Ship,** by *sh*.

ability	feasibility	specification	monogram

experimental	fundamental	partnership	ownership

NOTES: (a) After *t* and *d*, *ification* may be joined, as the absence of the blend clearly shows that *f* is a suffix sign.

modification	notification	edification	ratification

(b) In many words *ship* may be joined.

friendship	workmanship	hardship	authorship

117

139. Hood or Ward, expressed by *d*.

childhood   likelihood   homeward   downward

NOTE: In many words *ward* may be joined.

forward   afterwards   towards   backward

140. Acle, Ical, Icle, expressed by *k*.

tentacle   medical   classical   chronicle

141. Itis, expressed by *ts*.

appendicitis   meningitis   peritonitis   tonsillitis

142. Ulate, expressed by *u*. In forming derivatives, the other letters are added.

modulate   modulated   insulate   insulator

insulation   formulate   emulate   emulative

NOTE: In most words *ulate* and its derivatives may be joined with perfect safety.

speculated   speculation   speculator   speculative

GENERAL EXERCISE

willingly		nobility	
appallingly		sensibility	
strikingly		advisability	
meaningly		legibility	
soothingly		desirability	
warningly		affability	
pleadingly		qualification	
cheeringly		gratification	
iongingly		signification	
exceedingly		classification	
grudgingly		mortification	
Millington		indemnification	
Farmington		identification	
Warrington		certification	
Wellington		lettergram	
Harrington		phraseogram	
Rockingham		epigram	
Cunningham		cablegram	
plausibility		pilgrim	

anagram		livelihood	
sentimental		knighthood	
ornamental		statehood	
monumental		onward	
clerkship		upward	
apprenticeship		northward	
airship		southward	
township		eastward	
steamship		westward	
kinship		awkward	
warship		reward	
worship		article	
womanhood		clerical	
manhood		physical	
girlhood		psychical	
boyhood		musical	
hardihood		icicle	
motherhood		radical	
brotherhood		technical	
neighborhood		cuticle	

ethical		manipulation	
magical		populated	
nautical		articulate	
bicycle		articulation	
periodical		inarticulate	
gastritis		formulated	
stimulate		adulation	
stimulated		expostulate	
stipulate		regulate	
stipulation		matriculate	
cumulative		perambulate	
manipulate		speculate	

READING EXERCISE

WRITING EXERCISE

1. The classification and identification of the candidates proved to be an exceedingly difficult task.

2. If you have the essential educational qualifications, we can easily arrange for the certification.

3. The technical nature of the matter makes the work of the medical reporter very difficult.

4. An article on psychical research appeared in a recent issue of the periodical.

5. Every girl, when she reaches womanhood, should be prepared to earn her own livelihood even though there is no likelihood of her being called upon to do so.

6. You may matriculate in the college when you receive a notification of your eligibility.

7. The articles of co-partnership were drawn up according to the specifications.

8. The law stipulated that the statement of ownership should be published every six months.

EIGHTEENTH LESSON

143. -Rity, -Lity, -City, -Vity, -Nity, -Mity, with or
without a preceding vowel, expressed by *r, l, s, v, nt, mt*
respectively.

Arity, Etc.		Avity, Etc.	
popularity		depravity	
prosperity		nativity	
majority		brevity	
Ality, Etc.		**Anity, Etc.**	
brutality		urbanity	
utility		trinity	
frivolity		affinity	
Acity, Etc.		**Amity, Etc.**	
tenacity		calamity	
felicity		sublimity	
pomposity		proximity	

123

NOTE: In words ending with *ernity*, the reversed circle is used to express *er* before the suffix sign:

fraternity   eternity   taciturnity

144. -Stic, with a preceding vowel, expressed by *st*.

elastic   domestic   artistic   atheistic

145. -Tic, with a preceding vowel, expressed by *large circle*; -Tical, with a preceding vowel, expressed by a *loop*. In forming derivatives, the other letters are added.

politic   politics   energetic   energetically

hypnotic   systematic   systematical   systematically

NOTE: In many cases the *loop* may be joined.

political   theoretical   grammatical   automatical

146. -Ntic, with a preceding vowel, expressed by *n*. In forming derivatives, the other letters are added.

gigantic   authentic   frantic   frantically

147. Egraph, Igraph, expressed by *small circle* placed *over* the last character. A *loop* expresses *egraphy, igraphy.* In forming derivatives, the other letters are added.

telegraph	calligraph	telegraphy	telegrapher

148. Ograph, expressed by *o*. In forming derivatives, the other letters are added.

lithograph	autograph	photograph	phonograph

lithography	lithographer	lithographic	typography

NOTE: In most words *ograph* and its derivatives may be joined:

photography	stenography	stenographer	phonographer

149. -Logy, -Logical, with a preceding vowel, expressed by *o* (on its side, as in writing *ol*). The letter *e* is added to express *-logically, s* to express *-logist, n* to express *-logian.*

analogy	genealogically	geologist	pathologist

theology	theologically	theologist	theologian

GENERAL EXERCISE

singularity		technicality	
solidarity		vitality	
hilarity		mortality	
regularity		morality	
familiarity		fidelity	
sincerity		docility	
temerity		versatility	
priority		facility	
minority		futility	
authority		garrulity	
futurity		incredulity	
security		capacity	
alacrity		mendacity	
integrity		veracity	
reality		loquacity	
nationality		complicity	
rascality		publicity	
punctuality		elasticity	
criminality		passivity	

vicinity		romantically	
divinity		Atlantic	
femininity		calligraphy	
humanity		telegraphic	
Christianity		photographic	
extremity		photographer	
dignity		phonography	
journalistic		stenographic	
majestic		autographed	
statistics		biography	
automatic		mimeograph	
erratic		geography	
critic		geographical	
critical		hectograph	
critically		physiological	
pneumatic		physiologically	
phonetic		psychological	
despotic		biology	
theoretically		ornithology	
romantic		chronological	

doxology		entomologist	
tautology		phrenologist	
analogically		mythology	
entomology		philology	

READING EXERCISE

WRITING EXERCISE

1. The importance of punctuality and veracity cannot be over-estimated.

2. Tenacity of purpose and fidelity to the interests of the business were qualities which led to his rapid advancement.

3. In making a mimeographed copy of the tabulated report be sure to arrange the statistics in chronological order.

4. The professor of biology sent me an autograph copy of his book.

5. A knowledge of phonetics is an aid to the student of phonography.

6. In the capacity of athletic director the instructor of stenography showed great business ability.

7. We do not question his veracity, but it is necessary for him to go through the formality of filing a bond for security.

8. The stenographer should have a thorough familiarity with the spelling of important geographical names.

NINETEENTH LESSON

---

150. **Omission of Words.** The rules for the omission of words in phrase writing are of great importance, and should be carefully studied. We now give a few more illustrations.

in order to judge		for the time being	
in order to prepare		I would like to know	
in order to see		I would like to have	
on the subject		I am of the opinion	
question of time		kindly let us know	
sooner or later		bill of particulars	
little or no		thanking you for your attention	
little or nothing		do you mean to say	
in the matter			
in the market		in such a manner	
on the market		on account of the way	
up to the time		some time or other	

130

151. Intersection. The expedient known as inter-section, or the writing of one character through another, is sometimes useful for special phrases. In applying this expedient the writer must rely very largely upon his own judgment. In his daily work as stenographer or reporter, he may find some terms peculiar to the business in which he is engaged occurring so frequently that special forms may be adopted for them which will be brief and yet absolutely distinctive. Very often the intersection of one character through another will meet the exigency. The following are useful examples:

A. D.		Democratic party	
A. M.		Republican party	
P. M.		Progressive party	
C. O. D.		political party	
price list		Baltimore & Ohio (B. & O.)	
list price		New York Central	
selling price		Michigan Central	
market price		Illinois Central	
Chamber of Commerce		Union Pacific	
Board of Trade		Canadian Pacific	
Board of Education		Northern Pacific	
Board of Managers		Grand Trunk	

General Manager		inclosed blank	
Assistant General Manager		application blank	
endowment policy		order blank	
indemnity policy		Great Britain	
bank draft		bond and mortgage	
vice versa		Associated Press	

152. Indication of "Ing." *Ing-the, ing-that, ing-you, ing-your, ing-his, ing-their, ing-and, ing-this, ing-us,* is expressed by writing the word following *ing* in the *ing* position—just as *ington* is expressed by writing *ton* in the *ing* position.

doing the		knowing the	
doing his		knowing their	
doing your		knowing this	
doing their		working and	
doing this		having the	
giving the		having their	
giving their		having your	
giving you		coming and	
giving us		seeing this	
mailing you		wishing that	

153. Modification of Word Forms. As previously explained, the forms for certain words are modified to permit of phrase writing. The following are useful illustrations:

Week		Possible	
past week		as soon as possible	
last week		as near as possible	
this week		least possible delay	
next week		Early	
for the past week		at as early a date as possible	
for last week		at your early convenience	
for this week		at your earliest convenience	
for next week		at your earliest possible convenience	
Few		Sorry	
for a few weeks		I am sorry to hear	
for a few months		I am sorry to learn	
few weeks ago		we are sorry to hear	
few hours ago		we are sorry to report	
		we are sorry to say	
Ago			
year or two ago		I am very sorry	
many years ago		you will be sorry	

Esteemed

esteemed favor

your esteemed favor

esteemed letter

your esteemed let-
ter

I am in receipt of
your esteemed
letter

I am in receipt of
your esteemed
favor

we are in receipt of
your esteemed
favor

we are in receipt of
your esteemed
letter

Beg

I beg to acknowl-
edge receipt

I beg to inclose

I beg to thank you

we beg to acknowl-
edge

we beg to acknowl-
edge receipt

Mail

by this mail

by to-day's mail

by this day's mail

by return mail

by mail

by same mail

by early mail

Course

of course

of course it is

as a matter of
course

Fact

as a matter of fact

call your attention
to the fact

in point of fact

you are aware of
the fact

I am aware of the
fact

well-known fact

Sure

be sure

to be sure

you may be sure

we are sure		**Account**	
you will be sure		on account of that	
Please		on account of this	
please find inclosed		on account of my	
inclosed please find		on account of the fact	
please let us hear from you		**Thank**	
I would be pleased		thanking you for	
we will be pleased		thanking you for your attention	
Present		thanking you for your kind attention	
present time		thanking you for your favor	
at the present time		thanking you for your letter	
at the present moment		I desire to thank you	
on the present occasion		I have to thank you for	
Class		**Order**	
first-class		your order	
first-class manner		we have your order	
first-class condition		thanking you for your order	
Again		**City**	
over and over again		city of Chicago	
again and again		city of Boston	

Department

treasury depart- ment			
war department			
navy department			
post-office depart- ment			
state department			
police department			
fire department			
legal department			
inquiry department			
credit department			
shoe department			
furniture depart- ment			
purchasing depart- ment			
shipping depart- ment			
mail order depart- ment			

Company

and company

railroad company

express company

insurance company

transportation
company

telephone company

electric company

electrical company

trust company

Us

to us

write us

please write us

please wire us

kindly give us

Avenue

Washington Avenue

Wabash Avenue

Massachusetts
Avenue

Holder

stockholder

shareholder

policyholder

READING EXERCISE

WRITING EXERCISE

1. Gentlemen: As requested we are sending you a copy of our price list giving illustrations and full descriptions of all the articles we now handle. If you are in the market for anything in our line we should like to have our representative call on you with samples.

Thanking you for the inquiry and hoping to be favored with your order, we are

Very truly yours, (66)

2. Dear Sir: A few days ago we received a letter from you in which you asked us to furnish you with information about a firm in this city. We are sorry to report that this firm has never done business with us and that therefore we have no data in our files about it. We have heard again and again that these people are doing a good business and so far as we know their affairs are in first-class condition at the present time. We regret to state that we cannot give you further details.

Yours very truly, (99)

3. Gentlemen: Thank you for the order which has just been received. This order will be filled immediately with the exception of the second item. As our supply of this article is completely exhausted we shall be unable to ship for a few days. We trust that this arrangement will be entirely satisfactory to you and that you will not be inconvenienced by the delay.

Assuring you of our prompt attention at all times, we are

Very respectfully yours, (78)
243

TWENTIETH LESSON

INITIALS

A		H		O		V	
B		I		P		W	
C		J		Q		X	
D		K		R		Y	
E		L		S		Z	
F		M		T			
G		N		U			

154. It should be borne in mind that there is no context to initials. They should therefore be written with unusual care. Many writers prefer to write initials in longhand, and if this is done a great saving in time may be effected by writing them in small letters and joining the letters, thus:

A. B. Smith   C. D. Brown   E. F. Jones

139

STATES AND TERRITORIES

(The contractions used are those adopted by the Post-Office Department.)

Ala.		Ky.		Ohio	
Alaska		La.		Okla.	
Ariz.		Me.		Oreg.	
Ark.		Md.		Pa.	
Cal.		Mass.		P. I.	
Colo.		Mich.		P. R.	
Conn.		Minn.		R. I.	
Del.		Miss.		S. C.	
D. C.		Mo.		S. Dak.	
Fla.		Mont.		Tenn.	
Ga.		Nebr.		Tex.	
Guam		Nev.		Utah	
Hawaii		N. H.		Vt.	
Idaho		N. J.		Va.	
Ill.		N. Mex.		Wash.	
Ind.		N. Y.		W. Va.	
Iowa		N. C.		Wis.	
Kans.		N. Dak.		Wyo.	

PRINCIPAL CITIES

(Arranged in order of population, 1910 census.)

City		City		City	
New York		Jersey City		Memphis	
Chicago		Kansas City		Scranton	
Philadelphia		Seattle		Richmond	
St. Louis		Indianapolis		Paterson	
Boston		Providence		Omaha	
Cleveland		Louisville		Fall River	
Baltimore		Rochester		Dayton	
Pittsburgh		St. Paul		Grand Rapids	
Detroit		Denver		Nashville	
Buffalo		Portland		Lowell	
San Francisco		Columbus		Cambridge	
Milwaukee		Toledo		Spokane	
Cincinnati		Atlanta		Bridgeport	
Newark		Oakland		Albany	
New Orleans		Worcester		Hartford	
Washington		Syracuse		Trenton	
Los Angeles		New Haven		New Bedford	
Minneapolis		Birmingham		San Antonio	

155. The terminations *burg, ville, field, port* may generally be expressed by the first letter, joined or disjoined as convenient; and *ford,* by *fd.*

Harrisburg	Evansville	Williamsport
Fitchburg	Knoxville	Oxford
Danville	Springfield	Rockford
Zanesville	Davenport	Hanford
Jacksonville	Newport	Milford

156. A clear distinction should be made between *ton* and *town.*

Johnston	Johnstown	Charleston	Charlestown

157. The names of cities and states may often be joined.

Buffalo, N. Y.	Detroit, Mich.
Rochester, N. Y.	Baltimore, Md.
St. Louis, Mo.	Chicago, Ill.
Minneapolis, Minn.	Denver, Colo.
St. Paul, Minn.	Memphis, Tenn.
Washington, D. C.	Omaha, Nebr.
Boston, Mass.	Louisville, Ky.

158. When the words "State of" precede the name of a state, omit *of* and join the words, if convenient.

State of New York	State of Massachusetts
State of Nebraska	State of Pennsylvania
State of Illinois	State of Louisiana

POINTS OF THE COMPASS, ETC.

159. In certain lines of business the following forms will be found very useful.

north		northeast	
south		southeast	
east		northwestern	
west		southwestern	
northern		northeastern	
southern		southeastern	
eastern		northwest quarter	
western		southwest quarter	
northwest		northeast quarter	
southwest		southeast quarter	

GENERAL RULES

160. When the distinctive appearance of the primitive word-form can be preserved, it is allowable to join to form the derivatives.

favorable	careless	nameless

fable	kill	nail

161. If it should be found desirable to indicate with precision the short sound of any vowel, a small curve can be placed beneath the vowel.

minion	immigrate	onion	writ

NOTE: This expedient is seldom necessary. It is useful, occasionally, to make a clear distinction between words like *return* and *writ*, *emigrate* and *immigrate*, and between the diphthong $\bar{u}$ and $\overline{\imath u}$, as in *minion*

162. The following words are given to illustrate the importance of placing the second circle outside the line when two circles are joined.

namely	daily	payee	carry

nigh	die	pie	kind

163. There are a few infrequent words, consisting of several vowels in succession — usually Indian names — in which it is more convenient to write the letters separately, and to indicate their connection by drawing a line underneath.

Lehigh	ayah	yahoo

164. In the termination "n-ment" the jog between the N and M may be omitted.

assignment	consignment	refinement

discernment	adjournment	atonement

165. In the termination *gency*, the N may be omitted.

agency	contingency	emergency

exigency	urgency	cogency

166. A very easy and graceful blend may be secured by joining S to V without an angle in the termination *sive.*

expensive	expansive	offensive

extensive	defensive	intensive

167. The Scotch or German *ch*, the Irish *gh*, and the Welsh *ll* may be expressed by a dot over *k*, *g*, and *l*, respectively.

Loch	Ach	Lough	Llan

168. The contracted forms for *hundred* and *thousand* are employed only where these words are preceded by numerals, the article *a* or some such word, as *few*, *many*, *several.* Note the following.

KEY: Thousands of people visited the Exposition and it was said that hundreds were turned away.

Several hundred came to the convention. I have disposed of a thousand copies of the magazine.

READING EXERCISE

WRITING EXERCISE

1. In the United States, immigration always greatly exceeds emigration.

2. The election writs were correctly made out but the returns were far in excess of all expectations.

3. The laws in the state of New York differ from those in the state of Nebraska in this respect.

4. Almost daily many people are killed through the carelessness of agents of the electric railway companies.

5. The payee of this draft, Mr. J. M. Johnstown, is unknown to us and it will be necessary for him to be identified before we can give him the money.

6. The firm positively declined to accept the consignment of oranges from Florida. They claimed that this shipment had been damaged on account of the carelessness in nailing the boxes as well as by the unfavorable climatic condition during transit.

7. The urgency of the case called for emergency measures and the manager, Mr. R. K. Johnson, after an exhaustive study of the matter decided that the plan proposed by one of the agents, Mr. D. E. Hanford, is the only way out of the difficulty.

A Short Vocabulary

A

abundant

accident

accom-
    modation

address

adminis-
    trator

affidavit

amalgamate

amalgama-
    tion

America

among

amount

annual

another

anxious

appear

appearance

application

apprehend

approval

approve

approximate

arbitrary

architect

assemblage

attach

attorney

authenticity

authorita-
    tive

automobile

B

bankrupt

behold

benevolent

benignant

boulevard

C

cabinet

casual-ly

catalog

century

church

citizen

civil

civilization

coincide

comparative

conclusive

congregation

consonant

conspicuous

constant

cordial

corroborate

cosmopolitan

count

coupon

covenant	discover	executive
crucible	dispropor-tionate	exorbitant
cultivation	dissatisfac-tion	expedient
curious	dividend	**F**
D	doctrine	flour
danger	duration	fulfill
dangerous	**E**	**G**
deceive	earnest	generation
default	economical	glorious
defendant	election	glory
degenerate	engage	**H**
delegate	English	handkerchief
delegation	employer	headquarters
democrat-ic	enormous	hieroglyphic
demoralize	envelope	hitherto
deponent	equality	horizontal
designate	equivalent	husband
develop	etc.	**I**
disadvantage	evaporate	ignoran-ce/t
disaster	execute	illustrate

inclosure		legislative		**P**	
incoherent		legislator		parcel	
incompre-hensible		legislature		parliament	
indefatigable		likewise		partial	
indis-pensable		litigation		passenger	
inherit		logic		persecute	
instanta-neous		luxury		persevere	
instead		**M**		plaintiff	
institute		manuscript		practical	
institution		messenger		practice	
intend		misdemeanor		precede	
introduction		modern		prevail	
iron		**N**		procedure	
J		negligence		proceed	
jurisdiction		**O**		production	
juxtaposition		obedient		promulgate	
L		obligation		property	
laboratory		o'clock		prosecute	
legislate		operation		prospectus	
legislation				prove	

provoke		situation		United States	
punctuation		social		United States of America	
Q		specific			
qualify		specify		universe	
quarter		steady, study		unusual	
R		strengthen		**V**	
really		struggle		variety	
reason		stupidity		various	
reciprocate		subaltern		verdict	
refuse		support		versatile	
remunerate		sympathy		versus	
repugnant		**T**		vocabulary	
resignation		testimonial		vocation	
revolution		testimony		volunteer	
revolutionize		thankful		vote	
righteous		thermometer		**W**	
rule		thwart		warrant	
S		tranquil		warehouse	
salesman		**U**		wholesale	
secretary		unavoidable		withdrew	

SHORTHAND AS A MEANS OF MENTAL CULTURE

(For key, see page 154.)

SHORTHAND AS A MEANS OF MENTAL CULTURE

(Key to Shorthand Plate on page 153)

With shorthand every person may form his own books of reference according to his own requirements, and that in the same space as though they were printed; and no selection of printed books would contain and only contain what he wanted. Any person who will collect only for a brief time such facts into shorthand as appear likely to be useful in life, and sometimes read over what is so collected, will find the *ideas* secured again and again recurring in future reading. If this selecting be continued, it will come to be recognized that every newspaper or magazine article, and not a few of the so-called new books, are but a more or less ingeniously contrived patch-work of old ideas, though doubtless the writer in many cases believed them to be original; and the reader will end in knowing *ideas* apart from words, and will recognize them in whatever dress they may be presented, just as we know our friends by their features, however they may be attired. For ideas, as seen in print, heard in words, or felt in the mind, are much like the stars—many reflections of a few originals.—*C. R. Needham.*

Made in United States
Orlando, FL
09 March 2023

30858745R00095